SERVICE QUALITY OF HOSPITALS

SERVICE QUALITY OF HOSPITALS

Dr. P.N. Harikumar
Dr. Mathew George

ABHIJEET PUBLICATIONS
NEW DELHI 110002

ABHIJEET PUBLICATIONS
4658-A, First Floor, Ambika Bhawan,
21 Ansari Road, New Delhi 110002
Phone: 011-23259444
E-mail: abhijeetpublication@gmail.com
www.abhijeetpublications.com

SERVICE QUALITY OF HOSPITALS

First Published 2021

ISBN 978-81-953707-6-4

PRINTED IN INDIA

Published by J.K. Singh for Abhijeet Publications, New Delhi-110002, Lasertypeset by Abhijeet Typesetters, New Delhi and Printed at Milan Enterprises, New Delhi.

Preface

Service Quality is usually considered as the yard stick of customer's satisfaction. Satisfaction is a person's feeling of pleasure or disappointment that results from comparing a product's perceived performance (or outcome) to expectations. Tangible products usually show stability in quality but Services, especially those involving high labour; are heterogeneous, their quality and performance often vary from producer to producer, from customer to customer, The hospital industry in Kerala is growing day, by day and it has a number of categories and subcategories. The health sector in Kerala is broadly divided into Government and Private sector hospitals. Government sector hospitals include Medical colleges, District hospitals, Taluk hospitals, Primary Health Centres and others such as TB centres, Leprosy Hospitals, Women and Children Speciality, Mental hospitals and Community Health Centres. Private hospitals include Medical Colleges, Multi-speciality Hospitals, Super-speciality Hospitals, Clinics, etc. The quality of service showed a great variation among different categories of hospitals. This study attempts to analyse the satisfaction level in each category and the factors affecting the level of satisfaction among patients of different categories of hospitals. Most of the past studies tried to analyses the factors affecting a particular sector or area. A study on Service Quality covering hospitals in various sectors has not been conducted in Kerala. This study tries to analyse the various factors affecting the Service Quality of hospitals.

Authors

Contents

1

Introduction

1.1 Introduction

Service Quality is usually considered as an outcome of customersatisfaction. Satisfaction is a person's feeling of pleasure or disappointment that result from comparing a product's perceived performance (or outcome) to expectations. Service Quality has been defined as "the outcome of an evaluation process where the consumer compares his expectations with the service he has received" or the difference between expected service and perceived service. Parasuraman, Zeithaml, and Berry (1988) state that, "Service Quality is an abstract and elusive construct because of three features unique to services: intangibility, heterogeneity, and inseparability of production and consumption". Services are different from goods (tangible products) in terms of how they are produced, consumed, and evaluated. The quality of intangible service products, such as treatment in ahospital, experiences from stadium, resort, hotel or amusement park, is difficult to assess as in the case of tangible products. Tangible products usually show stability in quality but Services, especially those involving high labour are heterogeneous, their quality and performance often vary fromproducer to producer, from customer to customer, and fromday to day (Zeithaml, Parasuraman, & Berry, 1990). Another feature of service is that production and consumption of most services are inseparable (Zeithamlet al., 1990). In other words, quality of service is often seen during service delivery, usually in an interaction betweenthe customer and theprovider, rather than being engineered at the manufacturing plant, and deliveredintact to the customer (Zeithamlet al., 1990).

The quality of service is usually measured in two dimensions, technical and functional. Technical quality is defined primarily on the basis of the technical accuracy of the activities and procedures. Several techniques for measuring technical quality have been proposed and are currently in use in various service organisations. Functional quality relates to the manner of delivery of various services. The total Service Quality can be subdivided as Basic Service Quality (BSQ), Value Added Service Quality (VASQ), Critical Service Quality (CSQ).

A hospital is a health care institution providing patient treatment by specialized staff and equipment. The primary function of every hospital is patient care. As patients are the main users, the success of any hospital depends on the quality of services provided by it to its customers or patients. Quality of goods and services is accepted as an important factor that determines the demand from goods and services. Competitive advantage of firms also depends on the quality of its outputs. The term 'quality' in the service sector seems to be different from the term in the goods market. The quality of a commodity can be evaluated and expressed in absolute terms, but it is not possible in the case of the service sector. Service Quality has been defined as "the outcome of an evaluation process where the consumer compares his expectations with the service he has received" or the difference between expected service and perceived service.Perception is the process by which we select organize and interprets information inputs to create a meaningful picture of the world. Customers compare the perceived services with the expected services.

As the hospital has to serve different categories with different expectations, Service Quality studies of hospitals are mainly based on the satisfaction of patients or their judgment about Service Quality. The expectation regarding the quality of the service may be different to different people. Patients form service expectation from many sources such as past experience, word of mouth and advertising, etc.

The hospital industry in Kerala is growing day by day and it has anumber of categories and subcategories. The health sector in Kerala is broadly divided into Government and Private sector hospitals. Government sector hospitals include Medical Colleges, District Hospitals, Taluk Hospitals, Primary Health centres, and others include TB centres, Leprosy Hospitals, Women and Children Speciality, Mental Hospitals and Community Health centres. Private hospitals include Medical Colleges, Multi-speciality and Super- Speciality Hospitals, Clinics etc. The quality of service shows a great variation across different categories of hospitals. This study attempts to analyse the satisfaction level in each category and factors affecting the level of satisfaction among patients of different categories of hospitals.

1.2 Scope and Importance of the Study

Hospital business is growing day by day in Kerala. It is generally considered as a service-oriented industry. Hospitals in Kerala offer a wide range of services to their customers. The services may vary according to the type of hospitals.The important services provided by hospitals include: Out Patient Care, In-patient Care, Specialized Services (Dental, Ear, Nose and Throat [ENT]), Surgical Services, Maternity (Antenatal Care, Perinatal and Postnatal Care), Pharmaceutical Services, Laboratory Services, HIV/AIDS Counselling Services, Diagnostic Services (Laboratory, X-ray, ECG, Ultra Sound Scan), Outreach Services (Reproductive and Child Health, Family Planning, Students' Clinic), Catering Services (Canteen Facility), andMortuary services.

In modern days, most of the hospitals are turned into profit oriented ones. In this competitive world competition among hospitals is also increasing. In the era of competition, the main concern is for survival and competition. When the urge for profit increases, quality of services is sacrificed and the patients have to suffer a lot. Studies reveal the facts regarding the quality of services offered by different types of hospitals and the awareness level and satisfaction level of patients regarding the services offered by the hospitals. Hence, this study, focused, on the Service Quality of Allopathic hospitals in Government and Private sector in Kerala is relevant.

1.3 Research Gap

From the review of literature, it is clear that several studies have been conducted regarding Service Quality in various service sectors. But most of the studies are concentrated on the banking sector. However, studies regarding Service Quality are very rare in Kerala. In Kerala, hospital industry is growing day by day and there are a number of hospitals in various sectors ranging from Medical colleges to single room clinics. Most of the studies have only tried to analyse the factors affecting a particular sector or area. A study on Service Quality covering hospitals in various sectors has not been conducted in Kerala. This study tries to analyse the various factors affecting the Service Quality of hospitals. For the study, samples are selected from Government medical colleges, District Hospitals, Taluk hospitals and Primary Health centres in the Government and Public Sector and from the Private Sector, Private Medical Colleges, Multi-Speciality and Super Speciality hospitals were selected.

1.4 Statement of the Problem

Competition in the Hospital industry is growing at a vigorous rate in Kerala. As the competition increases the profitability of the hospitals is questioned. When profitability decreases some firms resort to unethical practices in the medical field, some medical practitioners also support these unethical practices. As the wealth ofthe population increases, the patients will become more quality-conscious and they will demand better services. The hospitals are generally categorised as Government Hospitals and Private Hospitals. The Government Hospitals are again classified as Medical College, District General Hospitals and Primary Health Centres. The Private hospitals may be classified into Private Medical Colleges, Multi-Speciality, Super Speciality Hospitals and Private Medical Clinics. The quality of the services may differ according to the type of hospitals. As the quality of services increases the cost also increases, because the private hospitals are charging a very high rate for better services. The service of Government and Public sector hospitals in Kerala are not up to the level. In the present scenario patients have to bear huge cost to get quality services from hospitals. This is not affordable to the common people in Kerala.

The main problem to be faced by the patient community in Kerala is the disparity in the quality of services offered by different types of hospitals. This study attempts to analyse the quality of services offered by different types of hospitals in Kerala. It also analyses the satisfaction level of patients regarding the services offered by the hospitals.

1.5 Objectives

1.) To analyse the factors influencing the selection of hospitals by the patients.

2.) To examine the most dominant factor that creates satisfaction among patients of Government and Private hospitals in Kerala.

3.) To evaluate the variations in the loyalty level leading to patient satisfaction in different hospitals.

4.) To analyse the impact of core services quality measures on the overall satisfaction of patients of Government and private hospitals in Kerala

5.) To find out the most dominant problem faced by the patients of both Government and Private hospitals in Kerala.

1.6 Hypotheses

1) There is no significant difference in the factors affecting the selection of hospitals by the patients of hospitals in Kerala.
2) There is no significant difference in the augmented facilities and care available for the patients of different hospitals.
3) There is no significant difference in the factors responsible for the satisfaction of patients of Private and Government hospitals
4) There is no significant variation in the mean scores obtained for the set of variablesdescribing the patient loyalty among various types of hospitals.
5) There is no significant dependence between overall satisfaction of patients and the core service factors such as Empathy, Responsiveness, Communication, Reliability, Access and Tangibility.
6) There is no significant difference in the factors responsible for the dissatisfaction of patients of Private and Government hospitals.

1.7 Research Methodology

The study is both descriptive and analytical in nature. It attempts to describe various Service Quality factors. Moreover, it analyses the Service Quality factors that affect the loyalty and satisfaction of the patients.

1.8 Data Sources

Both primary and secondary data have been used for the study. In the first stage of study, secondary data and literature were obtained from various books, journals, published and unpublished works, and the available medical publications. The primary data were collected by using a well-structured Interview Schedule distributed to the patients of Government and Private Sector hospitals.

1.9 Research Approach

Survey Research using a well-structuredInterview Schedule for patients of selected Government and Private Sector hospitals was adopted in the study

1.10 Period of Study

After a Review of Literature, a pilot study was conducted among 75 patients of Government and Private Sector hospitals for a period of two months, December 2018 and January 2019 and after testing the reliability and fixing the sample size the final Interview Schedule was administered to 550 patients for a period of 6 months from February 2019 to August 2019.

1.11 Research Instrument

A well-structured Interview Schedule was prepared with the objective of collecting all relevant information required for achieving the research objectives. The Interview Schedule was administered after conducting a pilot study and in consultation with an expert in Applied Statistics.

1.12 Population

The population includes the patients of Government and Private Sector hospitals in Kerala.

1.13 Pilot Study

A pilot study was conducted by using a draft interview executed among 75 patients of Government and Private Sector hospitals in Kerala.By analysing the information provided by the patients in the pilot study, the final Interview Schedule was drafted after conducting the ClassicalCronbach Alpha Analysis. Based on the Cronbach Alpha Model, the listed variables are found to be reliable.

Table 1.1 Cronbach Alpha Model of Listed Variables

Sl.No.	*Variables*	*Cronbach Alpha*
1.	Tangibility	.912
2.	Reliability	.963
3.	Responsiveness	.891
4.	Assurance	.951
5.	Empathy	.852
6.	Access	.862
7.	Courtesy	.911
8.	Communication	.896
9.	Personality Factor	.910
10.	Managerial Skill	.911
11.	Sustainable Services	.893
12.	Operation (Surgery) Facilities	.916
13.	Infrastructure	.892
14.	Information Technology	.886
15.	Price Fairness	.921

16.	Procedural Fairness	.966
17.	Outcome Fairness	.952
18.	Interaction Fairness	.895

Source: Survey Data

1.14 Sample size

After conducting the pilot study with the data collected from 75 patients, the Reliability analysis was conducted, and the Crombach Alpha of each variable was found to be greater than 0.7, which shows the high degree of reliability of the instrument used for the collection of data. The Interview Schedule includes 97 statements relating to Service Quality variables and another 15 statements relating to problems that may cause dissatisfaction, 16 statement relating to patient's loyalty and 13 factors relating to patient's satisfaction. As many as 141 statement relating to variables affecting satisfaction and Service Quality were used to determinethe sample size. The sample size is determined by the formula $n > (1.96s/d)^2$. Where 'n' is the sample size,'s' is the estimate of standard deviation, 'd' is the standard error of the estimate of the population parameter and the value 1.96 is the critical value from normal test at 5 per cent level of significance. The calculated sample size of 548 was the maximum of the sample size obtained from the responses of all the statements. Hence the sample was finally fixed at 550.

1.15 Method of Sampling

Two stage Random Sampling has been applied for the selection of sample patients. In the first stage, one hospital has been selected from each type of

Table 1.2 Hospital-wise Allotment of total sample size of 550

Type of Hospitals	Total No. of Hospitals	Selected	Number of patients as on 31/01/2019	Sample
Govt. Medical Colleges	11	Thiruvananthapuram	3, 600	120
District Hospitals	18	Aluva , Ernakulam	2160	72
Taluk Hospitals	81	THQH, Chavakkad, Thrissur	1440	48
Primary Health Centres	848	PHC Kollamkode, Palakkad	720	24
Others (TB Centres, Leprosy Hospitals, W&C Speciality, Mental Hospitals, Speciality (Others), CHC	286	CHC, Thottakkad, Kottyam	1440	48
Total (Government or Public Sector)			**9360**	**312**
Pvt. Medical College	24	MES Academy of Medical Sciences, Malapppuram	1440	48
Multi Speciality	31	MIMS, Kozhikkode	2850	95
Super Speciality	42	Malabar Cancer Centre,Kannur	2830	95
Total (Private Sector)			**7120**	**238**
Grand Total			**16480**	**550**

hospital and, in the second stage, the required number of patients have been selected proportionately from the list of patients who visited in the month of January 2019.

1.16 Methods for Analysis

Statistical methods such as Friedman Test, Kruskal Wallis Test, Mann Whitney U Test, Multiple Discriminant Analysis, Analysis of Variance (ANOVA), Multivariate Analysis of Variance (MANOVA), and Stepwise Multiple Regression were used for establishing the relationship between the variables under study.

1.16.1 The Friedman Test

The Friedman Test is a non-parametric statistical test developed by Milton Friedman. It is an alternative to the parametric repeated measures with ANOVA. This test ranks values from thelowest to the highest. The variable with the lowest rank is considered to be the most preferred one. Here, the test is applied to find out the dominant factor which influenced the selection of hospitals.

1.16.2 Multiple Discriminant Analysis

A Discriminant Function is a linear combination of the predictor variables that provide the best discrimination between the groups. The variables with high coefficients, and pooled within group correlation between discriminating variables and Discriminant function, are used to identify the important variables. As the first part in Discriminant Analysis, the Tests of Equality of Group Means is done to validate the power of each variable to the Discriminant function. Discriminant analysis is used here to find out the most critical factor that creates satisfaction among patients.

1.16.3 Analysis of Variance (ANOVA)

Analysis of Variance is used for examining the difference in the mean values of the dependent variable associated with the effect of the controlled independent variable after taking into account the influence of uncontrolled independent variables. In the study variation of Patient's Trust by their area of Residence is tested with the help of ANOVA.

1.16.4 Multivariate Analysis of Variance

To evaluate the variations in the Loyalty level of patients, leading to satisfaction, a Multivariate Analysis of Variance (MANOVA) was applied. The importance of MANOVA is seen widely in decisions related to a setof related variables observed in more than two groups. If ANOVAis used, it may give the result that a variable is not significant, but MANOVA may provide reasons to say that the variable is significant in the presence of all variables taken together. Also, while doing MANOVA, the real understanding of the possible variations become more pronounced. In the study MANOVA was aimed to analyse the response on such problems for explaining the possible deviations observed in patients of different hospitals. The MANOVA for this group of four factors, by types of hospitals and loyalty types, was considered. To explain the possible variations observed in these variables, in the different hospitals under survey, MANOVA for this bundle of four variables by one factor (type of hospitals) was considered. This procedure was to test the null hypothesis about the effect of factor variables on the means of the bundle of variables.

1.16.5 Mann Whitney U test

The Mann Whitney U Test, sometimes called the *MannWhitney* Wilcoxon *Test* or the Wilcoxon Rank Sum *Test,* is used to *test* whether two samples are likely to derive from the same population (i.e., that the two populations have the same shape). The Mann-Whitney U Test is used to compare differences between two independent groups when the dependent variable is either ordinal or continuous, but not normally distributed. The Mann Whitney U test is applied here to identify the difference in the augmented facilities provided by Government and Private hospitals.

1.16.6 Kruskal Wallis Test

The Kruskal Walis Test is a non-parametric test based on ranks. It is used to find out the differences between two or more groups of an independent variable on the ordinal or continuous dependent variable. It facilitates comparing more than two independent groups; so it is an extension of the Mann Whitney U Test. This test here examines the type of hospitals which provide more augmented facilities.

1.16.7 Multiple Linear Regression (Stepwise)

Multiple Linear Regression is a way of choosing predictors of a particular dependent variable on the basis of statistical criteria. The statistical procedure decides which independent variable is the best predictor, the second best predictor etc. Here the emphasis is on finding the best predictor at each stage.

When predictors are highly correlated with each other and with the dependent variables, one variable often becomes listed as a predictor and the other variable is not listed. Here, the method is used to find out the factors that create overall satisfaction among the patients of different categories of hospitals.

1.17 Limitations of the Study

1) The study focused only on Allopathic Hospitals, hospitals which are giving Ayurvedic, Homeopathic and other type of treatments are not covered in the study.
2) It is difficult to identify and collect data from a vast number of patients. So the study is confined to a limited number of patients.
3) There are various categories of hospitals ranging from Multi Speciality to single Room Clinics. The study is limited up to Super Speciality in the case of private sector hospitals.
4) The dominant factor influencing selection of hospitals may vary from hospital to hospital and the selected variable may not be relevant in the case of selected patients.
5) Most of the patients, especially with serious illness may not be in a condition to respond to the questions. This may affect the reliability of responses.

1.18 Scheme of Presentation

1) The first chapter contains the introduction of the topic, scope and importance of the study, statement of the problem, research gap,

objectives of the study, hypotheses, methodology, pilot study, sample size, method of sampling, methods for analysis, limitations of the study and chapterisation scheme.

2) The second chapter includes review of literature on service quality.

3) Theoretical Framework on Service Quality.

4) Factors affecting Service Quality in Government and Private sector hospitals in Kerala.

5) Summary of findings, conclusion and recommendations.

REFERENCES

[1] A.B.Sundaravadivelu (2013) Service Quality Strategies of Medical services - A study with reference to Private hospitals in Chennai, Published Ph.D thesis, University of Madras.

[2] Ansuman Samal (2018) Comparative Study on Service Quality in Public, Published Ph.D thesis, Siksha O Anusandhan (Deemed to be University), Bhubaneswar, Odisha.

[3] Lim, P.C. and Tang, N.K.H., (2003), "A Study of Patient's Expectations and Satisfaction in Singapore Hospitals", International Journal of Health Care Quality Assurance, *13* (7), pp. 290-299.

[4] Nishikant Waikar (2010), A study of Service Quality assessment in hospitals, Published Ph.D Thesis, Institute of Management studies, Devi Ahilya Vishwavidhyalaya, Indore.

[5] Parasuraman, V. Zeithaml and L. Berry, (1985) "A Conceptual Model of Service Quality and Its Implications for Future Research", *Journal of Marketing, 49* (Fall).

[6] Parasuraman, V. Zeithaml and L. Berry, (1988) "SERVQUAL: A Multiple-item for Measuring Consumer Perception of Service Quality," *Journal of Retailing, 64* (Spring).

[7] Sarhani Chakraborthy and Kein Frick (2013), "Factors Influencing Private Health Prider's Technical Quality of Care for Acute Respiratory Infection among UnderFive Children in Rural West Bengal, India", *Social Science and Medicine, 55* (5), pp.1579-1587.

[8] Syed Sadd Andaleeb (2008), "Determinants of Customer Satisfaction with Hospitals: A Managerial Model", *International Journal of Health Care Quality Assurance, 11*(6).

2

Review of Literature

Review of Literature provides a critical summary of research already done on related topics. Review of Literature is done to generate a theoretical and scientific knowledge about a particular phenomenon and results in a synthesis of what is known and unknown about that phenomenon. The primary purpose of literature is to gain a broad idea about the topic. Review of Literature facilitates selecting a problem and its purpose, developing a framework and formulating a platform for further study.

Many studies have been conducted from time to time at national and International levels to study the various aspects of service quality in various service sectors. A critical assessment of previous studies will make research more effective and will eliminate duplication and helps to find out the Research Gap.

This Chapter contains Findings of Researchers who had made earlier studies on Service Quality in various sectors. The Hospital Industry has undergone drastic changes in the recent years and competition is growing day by day. Mushroom growth has been reported in the hospital sector, but it has affected the Service Quality very badly. Hospitals become profit-making entities and they are less bothered about the quality of Services and the Satisfaction of the patients. Many of the Research Studies are done in Banking and Hotel Industry. But Studies are very rare in Hospital sector, especially in Kerala. A review of these studies is presented in this chapter in chronological order.

Parasuraman, A, Valarie A. Zenithal, and Leonard L. Berry (1988), Parasuram in his study developed a SERVQUAL model to analyse the Service quality. This model is later known as the GAP Analysis Model. The SERVQUAL model provides the management of service organizations with information about the organization's ability to provide quality service. He opines that customers form the perception of service quality according to the service performance they experience, and, based on past experiences of service performance.The service quality survey, using the SERVQUAL model, will assist the management to identify the respective organization's service strengths and weakness (GAPS) or it is the difference between the Expected and Perceived services.

Rosenstiel (1988), describes three prerequisites for general behaviour of employees towards customer orientation, viz individual knowledge, personal willingness and social allowance. In his study, he introduces following three dimensions of customer orientation, (a) Skills which the employee has got for being customer-oriented, (b) Motivation of the employee to serve the customers better, and (c) His or her decision making abilities and authority in the decision making process.

Lamber et al. (1990), conclude that employees who are highly qualified and have vast experience tend to be a bit reluctant in performing repetitive work, which decreases their focus from the consumers, the relationship between demographic factors and customer orientation is not that much explored and researches are still being done; so there is not enough of evidence regarding the demographic factors impact on customer orientation.

Narver and Slater (1990), define Customer Orientation as "organizational culture that most effectively and efficiently creates the necessary behaviours for creation of superior value for buyers and thus, superior performance for the organization." As per this explanation of customer orientation, we can say that it is an inter-functional coordination and cooperation which will help the organizations to attain a competitive edge over the competitors.

Cronin and Taylor (1992) in their study state that, increasing the economic level of service of the country will also increase expectations of the customers. Perception of customers plays a very significant role in identifying the Service Quality. Therefore, if a service organization wants to dominate in the present service-competitive environment, it must adopt strategies to deliver superior kind of services to its customers.

Ashok Shani and Hony (1992) in their study titled "Management of outpatient Services", make a detailed analyses regarding the guidelines of effective out-patient management and find that it results in cost reduction, less strain on hospital resources and satisfaction to the patients and relatives of the patients. It is estimated that thecost of one short-term inpatient is equal to 20 outpatient consultation cost. It leads to the popularity and acceptability of the hospitals.

Robort F Krampf and Darry W. Miller (1993), in their article "Hospital Successes and Failures" indicate change in Hospital Marketing, the suggested Framework observes that marketing and advertising have become an inevitable management function for hospitals during the yester years. A survey of hospitals states that the successes and failures depends upon the marketing strategies for the past two years. Then it depends upon the advertising and promotion programmes. They state that marketing activities that should be considered successful are designed to satisfy specific customer and physician needs and help the organization to adapt, in order to meet those needs.

Melvin F. Hall (1995), in his article aims to identify the parts of the servicedelivery system that are important to patients. He tries to find the delivery systems that can cause satisfaction. He suggests that hospital must find ways toimprove the efficiency of the service delivery system to achieve a corresponding increase inpatient satisfaction.

David P. Paul and Earl D. Honeycutt (1995), in their study, analyse marketing strategies and relationship strategies towards patients. They observe that the hospital had failed to address many of the patients'needsand wants in the health care market. They suggest that Marketing in hospital has to concentrate primarilyon advertising and public relations.

Gaba D, Howard S and Small S. (1995), in their study, they analyse the awareness level of the patients and the steps taken by the hospitals in creating this awareness. They suggest that situation awareness is critical inall areas of healthcare, especially in acute medicine and in procedures like anaesthesia.

Subramaniyam (1997) in his micro-study of Government community hospital in Kavali town, Nellore district finds that the right to health at the grassroot level h still been violated. He also states that the people in villages and small towns receive inadequate health care services due to corruptions of doctors as they are not service motivated. Inadequate infrastructural facilities and unhygienic condition also affect Service Quality. Awareness of the public along with committed progressive political leadership has been suggested by the study to overcome this situation.

Jeen Su Lim and Ron Zallocco (1997) have conducted a comparative study of hospitals and physician with the objective to ascertain the consumer attitude towards healthcare marketing. The study reveals that there is significant difference in consumers attitude towards the use and effect of various marketing practices provided by the hospital and physician.

Maria and Jose (2002) in their study find out that the service quality in hospitals has a significant impact on patient's emotions. Their results state that satisfaction of the patients involves diverse phenomena within the cognitive and emotional domain.

Seltman and Kent (2003), in their research identify the role of healthcare marketing professionals in patient's satisfaction. It further discusses the problems associated with tracking patient satisfactions and provide information on the function of the Medicare centers and Medical aid services. The study points out the views on medical healthcare leadership.

Thomas and Richard (2003), in their article entitled 'Treating patients like Customers', present their views on measuring patients satisfaction in the U.S. The study focuses on the developments in satisfaction measurement among hospitals and status of customer satisfaction measurement relative to other services. The study also analyses the role of healthcare organizations in measuring patient satisfaction and suggests measures for improving satisfaction level.

Marino and Phyllis (2003), in their research article entitled 'We Are the Voiceof the Customer' try to study healthcare marketing. They also explain the importance of meetingconsumer need. They also recommended ways to deal with consumers and analyse the attitude of patients towards medical care in detail. They have also tried to analyse its impact on their satisfaction level.

Dube and Laurette (2003), in their studypoint out the neglected angles of Patient–Centred Care. The Studydiscusses about how emotion affects patient satisfaction. It also stresses on the importance of targeting health information to specific segment of the audience. They also identify factors that could help patients to deal with their emotions. The study also recommends ways that makes them more receptive to healthcare information.

Johan Hellings, Ward Schrooten and Niek Klazinga (2007) have measured patient safety culture in five Belgian general hospitals. In the study they find that Safety culture played an important role in the approach towards patient's safety in hospitals. The dimensional positive scores in all hospitals were found to be low to average in all the hospitals. The lowest scores were for hospital management support for patient safety and non-punitive response to error. Although the same dimensions were considered as problematic in different hospitals, there have been variations between the five hospitals.

Eugine Fran, C, (2008), in his study, attempts to study the marketing aspects of both the private and the Government hospitals located in Kanyakumari district. He attempts to assess the socio-economic conditions of the patient respondents and to analyse the decision-making factors in the marketing of health care services. In his study he finds out that factors like 'pre-consultancy services' and 'quality of health services' play an important role in decision making. He also finds that the patients of the private hospitals have a better attitude towards core services when compared to the attitude of the patients of Government hospitals.

C. Jothi Baskara Mohan (2009) In his study he has tried to study the existence of the HRD system at the government hospitals in Tamilnadu and has found that they are rated only at a moderate level. The rate of the implementation of the HRD practices in the hospitals is also poor to moderate. The less experienced doctors are poorly perceiving above the HRD practices at the government hospitals than the experienced doctors. At the same time, they are viewing the constraints to implement the HRD practices. The study shows the importance of HRD at the government hospitals to satisfy their patients. Considering the investment made on the government hospitals by the welfare government, it should consider the welfare of the people (patients) and invest more on the implementation of the HRD practices at hospitals. The management of the HRD practices is equally important to enrich the service orientation among the doctors which will result in better patient care quality.

Anjali Patwardhan (2009) in her study tries to asses the effectiveness of consumer surveys on health services. She suggests that in the recent climate of consumerism and consumer focused care, health as well as social care needs to be more responsive than ever before. The consumer needs and preferences can be tracked by customaries and specific consumer surveys. Most researchers concentrate on consumer experience surveys rather than on just satisfaction surveys. It will help in identifying the specific opportunities for improvement and also in transforming them into strategic planning for improvement.

Koichiro Otaniand Fort Wayne (2009) have conducted a study to find out what influenced adult patients. For this data had been collected from one major academic hospital and four community hospitals. The study reveals that staff care and nursing care are the most influential factors. These two factors are found to be the distinctively stronger drivers of overall satisfaction than the other attributes like physician care, admission process, room, and food.

AleenaTasneem, Sundaes Shaukat, and Fatima Amin (2010), in their study entitled "Patient Satisfaction; A Comparative Study at teaching versus DHQ Level Hospital in Lahore, Pakistan" examine patient satisfaction with the treatment provided by the doctors. Satisfaction also depends on adequate equipment facilities, attitude of hospital staff and overall environment. Satisfaction of OP department and emergency department is also measured. The study notes that the level of patient satisfaction at teaching hospitals is overall good but less as compared to the results obtained at the DHQ level.

Nishikant Waikar (2010) in his study suggests, that patients define healthcare quality in terms of tangibles, reliability, responsiveness, assurance and empathy. The SERVQUAL model appears to be a consistent and reliable instrument to measure health care Service Quality. His findings show that SERVQUAL identifies key Service Quality shortfalls and is a more than sufficient yardstick to measure Service Quality in hospitals. The negative SERVQUAL scores (GAP-5) across all the dimensions shows that Service Quality should be improved. Healthcare managers should focus more on training the staff in order to improve the service delivery.

Prahlad Rai Sodani, Rajeev K. Kumar, Jayati Srivastava, and Laxman Sharma (2010), have conducted the Study on Measuring Patient Satisfactions. The study aims to know the perceptions of patients towards the public health facilities, choosing health facility, registration process, basic amenities, perception towards doctors and other staff and perception towards pharmacy and dressing room services. The study finds that most of the respondents were young and having low levels of education. It is also observed that thepatients are more satisfied with the behaviour of doctors and staff at lower health facilities compared to higher level facilities.

Sivakumar, M (2010) in his study attempts to analyse the marketing orientation of the hospitals and to examine the impact of marketing orientation of the hospitals on the perception of the patients on the hospitals. He also makes an attempt to evaluate the marketing strategies adopted by the hospitals. He concludes that the perceptions on the Service Quality of hospitals is higher among the rural patients than among the urban patients. The perception on the physician behaviour, supporting staff and atmospherics in hospitals are also seen to be higher among the rural patients than among the urban patients. The marketing orientation in the big hospitals is identified as higher than that in the small hospitals. The significantly influencing marketing mix orientation of the hospitals on the overall perception on Service Quality of hospitals is their product, price, people and physical evidence orientation. The important discriminant of marketing orientation among the big and the small hospitals are promotion and process mix.

YogeshPai, P., and Gaurav Ravi (2011), in their study, attempts to highlight patient satisfaction among the in-patients, during their interaction within the system in different phases of services. Services such as front office, food and beverage services, housekeeping services, discharge process, facilities provided by hospital, medical or clinical services and nursing services are analysed. The study concludes that health care providers should manage quality through a continuous redesigning process and should understand the factors that are highly associated with patient satisfaction.

Dr. Chandrakumar Sedamkar M (2011) his article entitled "Study of HealthManagement among the Aged", observed that about half of the respondents (out of400 patients) are found interested in health management through regular medical check-up, good food habits, dieting, physical exercises and Yoga. Among aged people, those who have pension or any financial aid have a more positive and favourable attitude towards health management than those who have no pension.

Anjali A Deshpande and Mahesh Kulkarni (2011) in their study "Telemedicine –A Ray of Hope for millions of Indians", states that Telemedicine is more important in developing countries like India. It allows extensions of medical usage to people residing in remote and rural areas where advanced medical usage may not beavailable. In rural areas, there has been an imbalance in healthcare. It has also become very difficult for patients to get a specialist's opinion in spite of spending time and money.

Raman Sharma, Meenakshi Sharma and R.K. Sharma (2011), they conducted astudy to assess the patient satisfaction level. Their objective is to know the behaviour and clinical care provided by the staff in terms of the amenities available. The results reveal that overall satisfaction regarding the doctor-patient professional and behavioural communication was high at almost all the levels of healthcare facilities. But, the study reveals that doctors have shown little interest to listen to patient problems. The services are very costly and are not affordable.

Srinivasa Rao (2011), in his study finds that most of the hospital services cannot be offered without the support of tangibles like interior decoration, lighting and ventilation, infrastructure like electricity, water, sewage, communication and transportation, security, etc. All the physical objects are used as evidence by the consumer to assess and expect performance from the hospital. Hence physical evidence plays a critical role in shaping consumer (patient) perception and also expectations. The physical evidence mix in hospital includes all the tangible representation of the service. The certifications and awards won by doctors of the hospital and the service certificates won by the hospital can all be displayed at the reception to instil confidence in the patients. Therefore, corporate hospitals should be very careful about presenting the right kind of atmosphere, which is both hygienic and relaxing; a large open lawn or garden with a simple layout and comfortable seating arrangement for patients has become essential for hospitals to remove the perceived risk of patients.

Rizwan and Hina (2011) in their paper "Assessing the Service Quality of Selected Hospitals in Karachi, based on the SERVQUAL model", find that there were gaps between patient's expectations and perception. Gap Analysis has disclosed large gaps in availability of informative brochures, error-free and fast retrieval of documents, waiting time and affordability of charges. These dimensions are spread out in all dimensions of SERVQUAL.

Ari Mawachofi and Stephen L Walston (2011) attempts to find out thefactors affecting nurse's perceptions of patient safety. They have examined 45 socioeconomic and organizational factors affecting patient safety and quality perceptions. They also reveal, nursing in these hospitals was dominated by foreign nationals. The high positive patient safety perceptions may be inclined by either individual or peer biases.

Mr. H. K. S. Kumar Chunduri (2011) in his research findings, he stresses that service quality is critical to the healthcare recipients. He observes that if hospitals meet all of the patients' expectations the patients would not be inclined to go to other healthcare institutions. He identifies various problems such as the lack of state-of-the-art technology, unprofessional employees, failure to deliver on promises, unsympathetic attitude towards solving patient's problems, services not being performed correctly, the first time, lack of insistence on error-free records, treatment timing not explained to the consumer, lack of prompt service, failure of employee behaviour to instil confidence, patients not feeling safe in all transactions, lack of consistent courtesy, employees not answering patients' questions, and hospitals not having patients' best interests at heart. The above issues influenced patients to seek other healthcare institution.

Suki, Lian and Suki (2011) analyse whether patients' perceptions exceed expectations when seeking treatment in private healthcare centres. A survey was conducted among 191 patients in the Klang Valley Region of Malaysia to measure the service quality of the private healthcare setting using SERVQUAL's five-dimension model. The results reveal that the customers' perceptions did not exceed their expectations, as they were dissatisfied with the level of healthcare services rendered by private healthcare centres. They felt that the waiting time to receive the service was excessive and that when there was a problem, the healthcare provider did not provide a fast response.

Brahmbhatt, Narayan and Nisarg (2011), in their empirical investigation of patients' perception on service quality adopting the SERVQUAL scale, indicated that private hospitals out-perform public hospitals. out of five dimensions, namely, Reliability, Physical aspects, Process, Encounter and policy, public hospitals perform better only in one dimension namely, Reliability.

Solayappan, Jothi and Sethu (2011), in their study "Quality Measurement for hospital services" adopted the SERVQUAL tool to investigate the perceptions and expectations of patients regarding hospital services in Chennai. The study finds that the service gap is very high in the case of reliability and assurance dimensions. They identified that the gap is the lowest for employee's willingness to help the patients. Huge gaps have been found in dimensions such as neat appearance, lack of interest in solving problems, communication regarding services, problem in doing the right things for the first time, giving services as promised, poor knowledge of employees and problems in personal attention.

Ahuja, Seema and Zehra (2011) in a study among Government and NGO eye hospitals in Haryana, India, analyse the service quality management using SERVQUAL model. The research discovers that the attributes of reliability and assurance have been identified by the respondents to be the most important dimensions of service quality. The responsiveness and tangibility dimensions shows a negative gap, implying that patient expectations of these two dimensions are not met by these two hospitals.

P.S. Kabaly (2011) in his study tries to identify the critical dimensions of service quality in hospitals from the perspective of Omani Medical Tourists and to develop an instrument to measure customer–perceived service quality in hospitals based on the identified dimensions with a specific focus on Medical tourists. He also tries to investigate the relationship between the dimensions of service quality and customer satisfaction. He reveals that the income level of the Medical tourists is not an influencing factor for visiting various tourist places of interest. He noticed that even people with lower income level show interest in visiting places. He also finds that respondents who have received treatment in different cities do not have shows any difference in their perception towards different quality dimensions

Sudha S.R. (2012) in her article "Private & Public Partnership in Healthcare Services in India" points out that public or private partnership would improve equity, efficiency, accountability, quality and accessibility of the entire health system. She suggests that public and private sector can potentially gain competitive advantage in the form of resources,technology, knowledge, skills, management practices and cost efficiency. The private sector can play an important role in transferringmanagement skills and the best practices to the public sector.

KirubaharanM. (2012)in his studys concludes that the prospect of the patients is very high in the case of Apollo Hospitals. The study applied the SERVQUAL model to assess settlement quality and featured the qualities and impuissance of the present level of convenience quality. He finds that there is a correlation between dimensions related to Service Quality and its variables of Perceived Value and that the Service Quality variables perceived and expected values are equal

Honkan G.G. Bagalkoti S. T. and Vaikunthe L. D. (2012) in their article "Utilization of Health Care Facilities in Haveri District", find that the incidenceof communicable diseases among the female membersin Haveri District is found to be higher compared to that among the male members. The major reasons for non-satisfaction about hospitals facilities include inadequate availability of equipment, improper treatment, lack of emergency services and timely treatment etc. They also find that accessibility of health care service to people is not uniform across all districts of Karnataka. The IPR (In Patient Ratio) found to be higher inrural areas for poorer households and for females. The SC or ST households have higherlevels of morbidity in the rural areas and nearly 60 percent of them used governmenthealthcare services.

RethinaSivakumar, G. (2012) in her study, examines the demographic and socio economic environments' influence on the different dimensions of Service Loyalty in Healthcare Services to find out the relationship between dimensions and Service Loyalty (Customer Loyalty) on Healthcare Services (Public and Private Hospitals) in Tamilnadu and also suggest a suitable strategic model for improving Service Loyalty. She finds that Patients Satisfaction is most significant predictor of Healthcare Customer Loyalty. The study also suggests that managements should ensure that the Healthcare Sector setting should concentrate on fair and prompt service to their consumers.

B. Hannah (2012) in her studies finds that the quality of treatment is an important factor for improving a patient's level of perception. The improvement in quality requires the participation and effort of the hospital personnel at all levels. Having high quality medical personnel is the key factor for improving the hospital's quality of treatment; the hospitals should improve the treatment and service skills of the personnel at various levels through training and by providing dedicated employees with timely reward which would be an effective method for hospitals to improve the quality in service and offer better treatment. The scope of services should be expanded. The hospitals and employees must understand the patient's needs, and position themselves in the patient's place, thereby to ensure the patients that they are sensitive to their needs.

Kumar and Chethan (2012) examine the Service quality at Apollo Hospital in Mysore, based on some dimensions of SERVQUAL. Four dimensions namely, tangibles, reliability, responsiveness, empathy were considered for the study. The results indicated that there is a significant difference between reliability and customer satisfaction. Responsiveness has had a positive influence on the patients' loyalty. Empathy and tangible dimensions have had a positive influence on the overall satisfaction of the hospitals' service.

Al-Borie and Damanhouri (2013) in their study measure Patients' satisfaction SERVQUAL model". Five public hospitals and five private hospitals were chosen for the study. It is found that the five dimensions of SERVQUAL (tangibles, reliability, responsiveness, empathy and safety) are reliable, valid and appropriate.

The results show that sex, education, income and occupation are significant in influencing patients' satisfaction.

Abousi and Atinga (2013) assess patients' hospital service quality perceptions and expectations using SERVQUAL and outline the distinct concepts used to assess patient perceptions through their study on "Service quality in healthcare institutions: establishing the gaps for policy action". The results indicate that patient expectations were not being met during medical treatment. Perceived service quality was rated lower than expectations for all variables. Contrary to the five-factor SERVQUAL model, four service quality factors have beenidentified in the study.

Francesa and Narayanan (2013) appraise the obstetric patient's expectations using SERVQUAL variables. The SERVQUAL measure was developed from the patient feedback and the results pointed to the service strengths as staff politeness, patient respect and privacy. Areas for improvement included cleanliness, women's involvement on decision making and communication.

Rina C Dave (2013) in her study findsthat Health care is undergoing fundamental changes. Proactive consumer culture has been created through new diagnostic and therapeutic techniques and technologies, information technology and a new generation of consumers. The influence of rising costs of health care and consumerism has resulted in significant changes in health care delivery. The expectations of quality care, efficiency, responsive service, ready access, fairness, and morale provider are a reality in all hospitals. High performance is essential in every healthcare process. The effective utilization of its resources is vital for every organization including Hospitals. Overall satisfaction level was seen in selected respondents regarding the hospital services especially in the case of Empathy, Assurance and Responsiveness dimensions of Service Quality. Respondents from multispecialty hospitals were more satisfied as compared to trust run and private hospitals. Respondents from the lower income group with higher education were more dissatisfied as compared to others. The dissatisfaction level was seen more in the South and Central zones as compared to West and North zones. The expectations of selected respondents were higher than their perceptions on selected private hospitals.

Sundaravadivelu A. B. (2013), in his study, concludes that the private hospitals are able to retain and convince their patients through their Service Quality strategies, and that their service are safe and efficient among others. Factors such as Personal attention, Amenities and clarity of services influence the patients to obtain satisfaction. With regard to perceptual difference, it is observed that every Service provider is after his patients. The Service providers have their own way of classifying their patients and grouping them to have a sectoral relationship for better management. The hospital staff in each type of Service more or less turn out to be campaigners and cheerleaders of their own concepts. It can be concluded that with regard to awareness of the patients of different services, the providers inform the service seekers about various schemes offered by them. The Service Quality strategies are just not a technology; it is a business strategy to select and manage the most valuable patients. It has become an increasingly critical means of developing and maintaining patient loyalty while also helping the business to achieve sustained profitability. Service providers can now manage every single contact with the patient to build long-lasting relationships and glean information and insights about patientneeds and their behaviour, to design and develop services, which helps to create value for the patients as well as the Service providers.

I. Irulappan (2014) in his study has found that in terms of service provision, private sector health care centres are better than the public sector health care centres. However, in terms of a few factors namely, Responsiveness dimension, Assurance dimension, Proficient medical staff and the Empathy dimension, Personal attention to work etc., public sector health care centres perform better than private sector health care centres. He concludes that there is a significant relationship between the socio-economic status of the customers and the various factors under perceived level of Service Quality.

Ramaiah Itumalla (2014) in his study; highlights the importance of Inpatient Service Quality and its relationship with patient satisfaction and loyalty in public and private hospitals. The HOSPITALQUAL, a scale for measuring the Inpatient Service Quality has been developed, based on three constructs, namely, Inpatient Service Quality, Inpatient Satisfaction and Inpatient Loyalty. And these constructs tested for the validity and reliability of the scale. The results show that Medical Service, Nursing Services, Supportive Services, Administrative Services, Patient Safety, Patient Communication and Hospital Infrastructure have a significant effect on overall Inpatient Service Quality.

Aghamolaei, Rafati, Kobra, Ahangari and Hoseini (2014), in their article, "Service Quality of a referral hospital in Southern Iran using SERVQUAL technique", view that Service Quality gaps are found in all Service Quality dimensions. The highest perception was in Assurance dimension and the highest expectation was in the Responsiveness and Assurance dimensions. The lowest perception was in the Responsiveness dimension and the lowest expectation was about empathy. It was found that the hospital was not able to meet patients' expectations completely.

Byju K.P.M (2014), in his study, tries to study about the healthcare services in BRICS countries by comparing major health indicators and to find out the Service Quality perceptions from the patients. He also tries to identify the Service Quality determinants which contribute (in the highest terms) towards overall satisfaction in private sector as well as public sector health care services. In his study, he comes to the conclusion that health indicators comparison, India is far below for competitors.

Bahadori, Mehdi and Ramin (2014) measure the quality of services provided to patients with chronic kidney disease in Kerman. The required data was collected using the SERVQUAL Interview Schedule containing the five dimensions of service quality. The results disclose that the means of patients' expectations were more than their perceptions of quality of services provided in all dimensions, which indicated that there were gaps in all dimensions. The highest and lowest means of negative gaps were related to empathy and tangibility. It was also found that only the difference between the patients' income levels and the gap in assurance was statistically significant.

Sritharan (2014) in his study titled, "Measuring service quality dimensions: an empirical study of private hospitals in Jaffna District, Sri Lanka" finds that the quality of hospital's services has had a significant impact on customer satisfaction of healthcare in private hospitals of Jaffna District in Sri Lanka. The objective of the study has been to assess the important dimensions of service quality in the services offered by private hospitals and to understand the factors that influenced service quality in private hospitals. Service quality was measured based on customer satisfaction levels by using an Interview Schedule which included the service quality dimensions of tangible, reliability, responsiveness, assurance, empathy, and communication. The research findings indicate that all factors have positive correlations and that the relationship among variables is significant. And further more Jaffna district private hospitals' patients rated the reliability dimension the most important of all, followed by tangibles, assurance, empathy, and responsiveness, whereas the communication dimension rated the least important of all.

Arasanamand and Khanchitpol (2014) analyse "The relationship between service quality and customer satisfaction of pharmacy departments in public hospitals" and also attempt to determine the influence of the five dimensions of service quality using the SERVQUAL instrument. The results testify that responsiveness and tangibles negatively impact customer satisfaction. When the five dimensions were separated, assurance had the greatest difference between average perception and average expectation (P>E), followed by empathy and reliability. There has been great difference between average expectations average perceptions (E>P) on responsiveness, followed by tangibles. This conveyed that the clients were dissatisfied with the service in terms of responsiveness and the tangibles of public hospital pharmacies.

Sabir, Wasim, Qaisar, Kamil and Khurshid (2014) evaluate the service quality in the military, public & private hospitals of Pakistan. By reviewing the different facts of quality management, this study analyses the use of quality of service i.e. the SERVQUAL model by which precision of the study was checked. Responsiveness, empathy, tangibility, reliability, and assurance have been the important determinants used in the study. The findings specify that private and combined military hospitals have been more anxious about quality of service but little attention has been paid on service quality dimensions by public health care centres. It is concluded that the service quality of military hospital and private hospitals is more satisfactory than that of public hospitals. People consider military hospital and private hospitals as a source to meet the requirements of patients due to timely treatment and other facilities. The patients are found to be worried about the condition of public hospitals. They are dissatisfied with behaviour of doctors in public hospitals. The environment at public hospitals was also not hygienic and healthy.

Amitabh Dey (2015) in his study suggested that the definition of fine dining has changed from the one associated with the French fine dining style, to one of a more relaxed atmosphere, over the centuries. He also suggests that diners perceive the service quality of the restaurant to be high when the service staff make the effort to understand and anticipate their customer needs and to delight them with personal touches. Therefore, restaurants should thus pay more attention to training and empowering their service staff to look for ways to make the dining experience a memorable one for their customers.

Aiswarya S (2015) In her study, observes that the first and foremost objective of all kind of healthcare units is to improve their quality standard to ensure patient satisfaction. Service Quality in health care can be put as the result from the comparisons between patient expectations about the service they will receive and also their perceptions about the service provider. Amended RATERAP dimensions can be used formeasuring patient satisfaction in the Indian context. Though quality plays a vital role in hospitals, no uniform policies could be designed for all the categories of hospitals. But patients basically seek effective communication with treating doctors and nurses which emphasizes the giving of adequate time and discussing the patients details, individualattention, courtesy and politeness, and listening to the patients sympathetically and reassuring them. Hence from the patients' perspective, the quality of care includes not only the service provided by the doctors or nurses alone, but, as a whole the quality of caring associated with it. Welltrained competent doctors, empathetic nurses and staff members and courteous and polite hospital personnel can comfort patients and consequently improve patients' satisfaction. In her opinion health care need to be patient-centric.

Somnath Chatterjee (2015) has scrutinized the health-seeking behaviour of the health service consumers and access of a healthcare service provider.

The study attempts to recognize the aspects in deciding patients access of healthcare provider in the district of Burdwan in the state of West Bengal. The statistical analyses identify the factors which are involved in determining the access to the healthcare provider by the patients. The study identifies that economic status, the education level of the patients, the income of the patient as well as presence of good doctors, proximity of the healthcare provider, infrastructure of the hospitals, coverage under employment scheme etc., are the prevailing bases for the access of the healthcare institution by the patients. Chatterjee concluded that patient satisfaction is not the main objective to get a competitive advantage among rival healthcare service providers; rather it leads to better patient care and service.

K. Nithyanandam (2015), in his study tries to analyse the History and Evolution of the Insurance sector in India and to understand the expectation and perception of customers towards the service quality of Life Insurance Corporation of India in Chennai. It also analyses the post-purchase behaviour of customers towards the Products and Services of Life Insurance Corporation of India in Chennai. He tries to generate a suitable model for maximizing the customer satisfaction through service quality. In the study, it is inferred that Responsiveness & Communication, Technology & Infrastructure and Courtesy & Understanding are the top three factors for male and female respondents with respect to the perception on service quality. He has also found that unmarried respondents have a little more satisfaction regarding the various aspects of Service Quality

Sindhya R (2016) in her study, she identified that patients' intention to avail the hospital services is the major concern for the hospital service providers. She suggested that Retention of patients is important and inseparable for the survival and sustainability of the hospital in the competitive environment. She has also found that, there are a number of public hospital people prefer private hospitals, because they offer good service. Even, if the cost of service is high people prefer to go to private hospitals because of favourable perception of reliability and tangibility.

Manoj Kumar (2016) in his study finds that the perception of management in organized retail outlets is higher than that of the expectations of the customers. It means that the organized retail outlets (Management) do not have a clear idea about the customer's expectation and that the delivery of services is not proper. Perception of management in the unorganized retail sector is on lower side in physical aspect dimensions and the expectation of customers are on the higher side. He also suggests that organizations should ensure that information regarding products and service are true and practical to reduce the gap and to gain the confidence of the customers. False or wrong information about products and service may break the credibility and image of the retail outlets.

V. Andal (2016) in his study finds that customer relationship quality variables are highly correlated with the other variables indicating that the customer expectations highly influence hospitals and healthcare centres. He confirmed that the most discriminating factor affecting Service Quality is patients' health-caring satisfaction and the second most important factor is hospital environment.

Pragati Chadda (2017) in her findings suggests that there are many other factors influence patient satisfaction with the medical services. Hospital emergency room, physician services and accommodations influence patients. Ease of getting medical care in multispecialty hospitals of Haryana, Chandigarh and Punjab has also been found to influence patients. Another influencing factor is the medical knowledge of the nursing staff.

R. David Rajesh (2017), in his study, concludes that the important SERVQUAL factors are tangibility, reliability, responsiveness, assurance, empathy, access, courtesy and communication. The core Service Quality in hospital industry has a significant impact on the facilities offered by the hospital industry. Both the Core and FIH have a significant positive impact on patient's satisfaction. The degree of satisfaction is identified as higher among the private hospitals compared to that of the Public and Corporation hospitals. Even though Service Quality and service fairness have a significant impact on the patient's satisfaction, the degree of impact on patient loyalty in less. The patient loyalty is very poor among the Public hospital whereas it is very highamong the Private and Corporation hospitals. Hence, the linkage between Service Quality, service fairness, patient's satisfaction and the patient loyalty has been proved in this research work. The important factors considered to be enriching the quality of hospitals are nurse's attitude, courtesy, easy access, communication and accounting. Since the level of expectations with regard to these aspects is differing among the Public, Private and Corporation hospitals, the hospital administration has to formulate the appropriate strategy to satisfy all patient categories.

Mr. Jaswal Ashish Rajendra (2017), in his study attempts to study the scenario of the healthcare sector in general and of the private hospitals in particular those are operational in Ahmednagar District and to study the patient expectation from private hospitals with regard tovarious parameters of Service Quality. He also tries to identify the patient perception regarding the Service Quality and facilities provided by private hospitals. He identifies that patients in private hospitals have very high expectations with regard to every service attribute and interestingly, the percentage of patients who have such higher expectations is substantial. The higher expectations of patients further warrant attention from the hospital administration that can incept steps to meet these expectation and the mammoth work and efforts required by them.

S.P. Murugan (2017), in his study tries to review the growth and development of healthcare services in India in general and Coimbatore in particular and to study the factors considered by the patients in choosing the particular hospital for availing the healthcare services. He also tried to analyse the satisfaction of patients on the CRM strategies practiced by the health care providers. Attempt has also beenmade to measure the patients' expectations and perceptions of medical services in the competitive healthcare system. He finds that most of the patients havefaced the problems of high cost of treatment and also majority of the patients are recommending the private multi-speciality hospitals to others.

Ansuman Samal (2018) observes that the comparative score for Service Quality was higher amongst the people visiting the private sectorhospitals whereas the cost factor is the major attribute affecting people visiting the public hospitals. He also observes that neither the public nor the private hospitals were able to match the expectations of the customers visiting them. Another finding is thatthe pricing of various health services available at the private hospitals is expensive. He concludes that private hospitals provide better positive feelings than the public hospitals.

Monisha (2018) the main object ofher study was to know the important factors which influence the service quality satisfaction of the bank customers. She observes that out of the factors influencing the perception of customers, the significant factors are understanding, security, courtesy, reliability, credibility, competence, tangibility, communication and access. The study considers the factors for knowing the perceived satisfaction of the customers. It is revealed from the study that customers were more satisfied with the e-banking service of HDFC.

Rupal Kantilal Khambhati (2018) in his study makes an attempt to identify the factors contributing to healthcare service quality and to study the impact of service quality perceptions on patient satisfaction and behavioural intention. The study concludes that expectations and perceptions of urban and rural patients differ for various items or variables. The study gap analysis shows a considerable gap between expectations and perceptions of consumers, which indicates that there is a difference in the expectations and perceptions of patients.

Dogra, Ajay Kumar (2019), in his study, attemptsto examine the Service Quality practices and customer orientation practices existing in selected public and private multi-specialty hospitals in North India. Responses and perception of the patients are analysed to find out the relationship between customer orientation and Service Quality. In the study he finds that there was a significant and strong positive correlation between Service Quality dimensions of nursing services and customer orientation. He also suggests that the patient communication dimension of Service Quality is one of the important attributes, which determines the Service Quality in the case of hospitals.

Glady Eswara Raj, S (2019), in her study attempts to find out the level of patient satisfaction towards the Government and Private hospitals and to analyse the facilities and services provided by the Government and private hospitals as alsoto know the problems faced by the patients in Government and private hospitals. In this study, the researcher focuses on the patient's attitude towards the hospitals in Tirunelveli district. It is observed that the patient's attitude,while selecting health service providers is based on the demographic and socio-economic status of the patients. She also observes that lower income patients and female patients especially for maternity are utilizing the services of Government hospitals due to the affordability and accessibility. In the case of private hospitals upper middle income groups, male, Government employees, professionals are utilizing their services due to the convenient consultation time, and approachable behaviour of front line staff and physicians.

Nidhi Malik (2019) The study reveals the fact that the service quality of polytechnic institutions can be explained through five dimensions of service quality, which are tangibility, responsiveness, empathy, reliability and assurance. The researcher findsthat some factors are not significant for overall perceived and expected service quality. It has also been concluded that due to various intangible factors and dynamic human behaviour, the quality of service is difficult to measure. In this study an effort has been made to analyse the perception and expectations of students in respect of service quality provided by government and private polytechnic institutions in Haryana. It has been concluded that student's perception levels are individually different in both types of institutions. It is also found that there is no significant difference in the services provided by the government and private polytechnic institutions.

In this chapter, totalseventy fivereviews have been made from Ph.D, theses, journals and reports both at national and international levels. The review makes it clear that researchers made varied attempts to get in the core of the construct. The review is in no way complete. The review of the above studies enables the researcher to find out the research gap and formulate the present studies. The studies reviewed reveal that no attempt has been made to analyses theServiceQuality, Level of patients' satisfaction with health care services and problems faced by patients of allopathic hospitals in Kerala. In order to fill this gap, the present study has been undertaken and to throw new insight into existing literature. In this context, the study attempts to analyse the Service Quality of Hospitals in Kerala.

REFERENCES

[1] Aaron A. Abuosi and Roger A. Atinga, (2013) "Service Quality in healthcare Institutions: Establishing the gaps for policy action", International Journal of Health Care Quality Assurance, *26* (5), pp. 481–492.

[2] Ahmed, Rizwan & Sameera, Hina, (2011) Assessing the Service Quality of selected hospitals in Karachi, based on SERVQUAL model. Pakistan Business Review, July 2011, pp. 266-314.

[3] Ahuja, Markanday; Mahlawat, Seema (2011); "Masood, Rana Zehra, (2011), Study on Service Quality Management with SERVQUAL Model: An Empirical Study of Government/ NGOs hospitals in Haryana", Indian Journal of Communication and Management Studies, *11*(2), (March 2011) pp. 310-318.

[4] Aiswarya S, (2015) Impact of Service Quality on Customer Satisfaction In the Health Care Sector (With Reference to Hospitals in Bangalore), Published Ph.D Thesis SRM University.

[5] AllenaTasneem, Sundas Shaukat, Fatima Amin,*(2010)* "Patient Satisfaction; A Comparative Study atTeaching versus DHQ Level Hospital in Lahore, Pakistan". Journal of Pharmaceutical Sciences and*Research, 2 (11) pp 767-774, ISSN.09 75-1459.*

[6] Amitabh Dey (2015) Assessing the Quality of Service and Delivery Standards: A Study of Selected Upscale Restaurants in Kolkata, Published Ph. D Thesis, School of Tourism & Hospitality Services Management (SOTHSM) Indira Gandhi National Open University, New Delhi.

[7] Anjali Patwardhan (2009), A Retrospective on Access to health care; International Journal of Health Care Quality Assurance 20 (6), 2007 pp. 494-505 Emerald Group Publishing Limited.

[8] Ansuman Samal (2018), Comparative Study on Service Quality In Public Vs Private Medical College Hospitals, Published Ph.D Thesis, Siksha O Anusandhan (Deemed University), Bhubaneswar, Odisha.

[9] Arasanamand, Prachayaporn and Yousapronpaiboon, Khanchitpol, (2014), "The relationship between Service

Quality and Customer Satisfaction of pharmacy departments in Public hospitals". Journal of Basic and Applied Science Research, *4* (1), pp. 144-151.

[10] Ari Mawachofi and Stephen L. Walston (2011), "Factors affecting Nurses' Perceptions of patient safety", International Journal of Health Care Quality Assurance, *24* (4), pp. 274-283.

[11] Ashok Sahni and Prof. Hony, (1992) "Management of Outpatient Services", Hospital and Health Administration, Second edition, Yem Yes Printers, Bangalore, 1992, p 18.

[12] B. Hannah (2012) A Study on Service Quality Of Government Hospital And Mission Hospital In Tiruchirapalli, Tamilnadu, Published Thesis, Bharathidasan University.

[13] Bahadori, Mohammadkarim; Raadabadi Mehdi; Jamebozorgi, Majidheidari; SalesiMahmood and Ravangard, Ramin (2014), Nephro Urology Monthly, Nephrourolmon. Sept; *6* (5).

[14] Brahmbhatt, Mamta; Baser, Narayan and Joshi, Nisarg, (2011), "Adapting SERVQUAL scale to Hospital services: An Empirical investigation of patients' perceptions of service quality". ZENITH International Journal of Multidisciplinary Research, *1*(8), pp. 27-42.

[15] Byju, K. P. M (2014), Service Quality in Healthcare: A comparative study of Private and Public sector healthcare services, Published Ph.D Thesis, Pondicherry University.

[16] C. Jothi Baskara Mohan, (2009). A Study of Human Resource Development Practices and Patient Care Quality in Health Care Services with Special Reference to Government Hospitals in Tamilnadu, Published Thesis, Madurai Kamraj University.

[17] David, P. Paul and Earl, D. (1995). "An analysis of the*hospital Marketing Relationship in the health*care industry" *The Journal of Healthcare Marketing, 10 (1), pp 35-49.*

[18] Dogra, Ajay Kumar (2019), Customer Orientation and Service Quality Practices in hospital industry, a study of Public and Private hospitals in North India, Published Thesis, Panjab University, Chandigarh.

[19] Dr.Chandrakumar Sedamkar, (2011) "Studyof Health ManagementAmong the Aged". Southern Economist, 49 *th year of publication, 49 (21), March 1, 2011, pp. 38-42.*

[20] Dube and Laurette (2003), What's missing from Patient – Centered Care?, Marketing health services, Spring 2003, 23 (1), pp 30.

[21] Eugine Franco. C, (2008), Marketing of Professional Services with particular reference to hospitals in Kanyakumari district, Published Ph.D Thesis, Manonmaniam Sundaranar University.

[22] Francesca, Garrard, Harini Narayan, (2013) "Assessing Obstetric patient experience: a SERVQUAL Interview Schedule", International Journal of Health Care Quality Assurance, *26* (7), pp. 582–592.

[23] Gaba, D., Howard S. & Small, S. (1995) Situation awareness in anaesthesiology. Human Factors, pp. 20-31.

[24] Glady Eswara Raj S (2019) Patients perception towards the services provided by the hospitals of Tirunelveli District. Published Ph.D. Thesis, Manomanian Sundaranar University.

[25] Hofmann, M. and Von Rosenstiel, L. (Eds), (1988), Motivations Management in Functional Management, Springer, Berlin, pp 14-19.

[26] Honkan, G. G., (2012)*Southern Economist, Golden Jubilee year of publication, 50* (9), Feb1, 2012, pp. No.31 -36.

[27]Hussein M. Al Borie, and Amal M. Sheikh Damanhouri, (2013) "Patients' Satisfaction of Service Quality in Saudi hospitals: a SERVQUAL analysis", International Journal of Health Care Quality Assurance, *26* (1), pp.20 – 30.

[28] I. Irulappan (2014) Service Quality in Health Care Centres: A Comparative Study between Government and Private Sector Hospitals in Dindigul, Published Thesis, Madurai Kamaraj University.

[29] Jeen Su Lim and Ron Zallocco (1997) "Consumer Attitude toward Health Care Marketing Practices: Acomparison of hospitals vs physicians", *The Jounal of Healthcare Marketing 12 (1),* pp. 91-108.

[30] Johan Hellings, Ward Schrooten and Niek Klazinga(2007), "Challenging patient safety culture: survey results" International Journal of Health Care Quality Assurance *20* (7), 2007 pp. 620-632.

[31] Jr. J. J. Cronin and S A. Taylor (1992). Measuring Service Quality: A Re-examination and Extension. Journal of Marketing, *56* (3), pp. 55-68.

[32] K. Nithyanandam (2015) Service Quality of Life Insurance Corporation of India, Published Ph.D Thesis, University of Madras.

[33] Kirubaharan. M (2012), A Study on the Quality of Healthcare Service and Patients' Satisfaction towards Apollo hospitals in Tamilnadu, Published Thesis, Bharathiaruniversity, Coimbatore.

[34] KoichiroOtani and Fort Wayne (2009) "Patient Satisfaction: Focusing on "Excellent" ".Journal of healthcare management pp 93-102.

[35] Kumar Chunduri (2011), The Service Quality Gap Analysis– A Study On Selected Hospitals in Hyderabad, Published Thesis AcharyaNagarjuna University, Andhra Pradesh.

[36] Kumar, Arun; Manjunath, Chethan, (2012), "Service quality at Hospital- a study of Apollo Hospital in Mysore", IOSR Journal of Business and Management, *4* (I), (Sept-Oct 2012), pp. 01-07.

[37] Lamber, D.M., Marmorstein, H. and Sharma, A. (1990), "The Accuracy of Salespersons Perceptions of Their Customers: Conceptual Examination and an Empirical Study". Journal of Personal Selling & Sales Management, *10* (8), pp 1-9.

[38] Manoj Kumar (2016) Service Quality Gaps in Retail Outlets in Haryana, Published Thesis Guru Jambheshwar University of Science & Technology.

[39] Maria Helena Vinagre and Jose Neves (2002), "The Influenceof Service Quality and Patients' Emotion on Satisfaction", International Journal of Health Care Quality Assurances, *21* (1), pp. 87-103.

[40] Marino and Phyllis, B. (2003), 'We Are the Voice of the Customer', Marketing Health services, summer*2003, 23 (2), p 52.*

[41] Melvin F. Hall (1995) "Patient satisfaction of aequiscence" The Jounal of Healthcare Marketing, *15.*

[42] Monisha (2018) Customers' Perception of Quality Delivery of E-Servicesin Banks, Published Thesis, MaharshiDayanand University Rohtak.

[43] Mr. Jaswal Ashish Rajendra (2017). A study on consumer's perception towards Service Quality in private hospitals. Published Ph.D. thesis, Savitribai Phule University, Pune.

[44] Ms. Anjali A Deshpande (2011) "Yeshwant Rao Chavan Maharashtra Open University, Nashik, Telemedicine-A Ray of Hope for Millions of Indians", Southern Economist, 50 (6), July 15, 2011, pp. 35-38.

[45] Narver. J. & Slater, S. (1990). "The Effect of a Market Orientation on BusinessProfitability", *Journal of Marketing*, 54(4), pp 20-35.

[46] Nidhi Malik (2019), Service Quality in Technical Education System: A Study Of Polytechnics In Haryana, Published Thesis, MaharshiDayanand University, Rohtak.

[47] Nishikant Waikar (2010), A Study of Service Quality Assessment in Hospitals, Published Ph.D Thesis, Institute of Management Studies, Devi AhilyaVishwavidhyalaya, Indore.

[48] Norazah Mohd Suki; Jennifer Chiam Chwee Lian and Norbayah Mohd Suki, (2011) "Do Patients' Perceptions exceed their expectations in Private Healthcare settings?" International Journal of Health Care Quality Assurance, *24* (1), pp. 42–56.

[49] P.S. Kabaly (2011) Medical Tourists' Perception Of Service Quality In Indian Hospitals: A Study With Specific Reference to Sultanate of Oman, Published Ph.D Thesis, Alagappa University.

[50] Parasuraman, A., Valarie A. Zeithaml, and Leonard L. Berry (1988), "SERVQUAL: A Multiple-item Scale for Measuring Consumer Perceptions of Service Quality," Journal of Retailing, 64/1 (Spring), pp 12-40.

[51] Pragati Chadda (2017), Service Quality and Patient Satisfaction with Reference to Multi Specialty Hospitals. Published thesis Kurukshetra University, Kurukshetra.

[52] Prahlad Rai Sodani, Rajeev K. Kumar andJayatiSrivastava, (2010) "Measuring Patient Satisfaction. A case study to improve quality of care at public health facilities". Indian Journal of Community Medicine.

[53] R. David Rajesh (2017) A Study on Linkage between Service Quality, Service Fairness and Service Loyalty in Hospitals in Madurai, Published Thesis, Periyar University.

[54] Raja Irfan Sabir; Nabila, Noor; Wasim, Ahmad; Farhan, Qaisar; Hussnain, Kamil andNaima, Khurshid; (2014), "Impact of Service Quality on Patient's Satisfaction using

SERVQUAL: A comparison of Combined Military, Private and Government Hospitals of Pakistan", Journal of Basic and Applied Scientific Research, *4* (1), pp 144-151.

[55] Ramaiah Itumalla (2014) Evaluation of Service Quality Management in Indian Hospitals: A Study of Select Hospitals Published Thesis, University of Hyderabad.

[56] Raman Sharma, Meenakshi Sharma, R.K. Sharma.(2011) "The Patient Satisfaction Study in a MultiSpecialty Tertiary Level Hospital, PGIMER, Chandigarh, India". Leadership in Health Services. *24*(1); 2011 pp. 64-73.

[57] Rethina Sivakumar, G (2012) A Study on Mediating Effects on Service Loyalty on Healthcare Services in Tamilnadu India, Published Thesis Bharathidasan Institute of Management.

[58] RinaC.Dave, (2013) Service Quality and Customer Satisfaction In Health Care Sector: An Empirical Study on Selected Private Hospitals of Gujarat. Published Thesis, Sardar Patel University, Vallabh Vidyanagar.

[59] Robert F. Krampf. & Darryl W. Miller (1993), "Hospital Successes and Failures Indicate Change in Hospital Marketing", Journal of Hospital Marketing *7* (2), pp. 11-19.

[60] Rupal Kantilal Khambhati (2018) Service Quality Measurement of Public Healthcare Facility: A Comparative Study on Urban and Rural Consumers of Surat District, Published Thesis, Gujarat Technological University Ahmedabad.

[61] S.P. Murugan (2017) A Study on Patients' Awareness, Satisfaction And Quality Measurement of Health Care Services Provided By Private Multi – Speciality Hospitals In Coimbatore District, Tamil Nadu Published Ph.D Thesis, Periyar University, Salem.

[62] Seltman & Kent (2002), 'The Final Word on Patient Satisfaction' Marketing Health services, Summer 2002, *23 (2)*, p. 3.

[63] Sindhya, R. (2016) Evaluation of Patients' Expected and Perceived Quality of Hospital Services Using SERVQUAL Approach in Southern Part of Tamilnadu, Published Thesis, Anna University.

[64] Sivakumar, M. (2010). A study on Evaluation of Healthcare services in corporate hospitals with special reference to Madurai, Published Ph.D Thesis, Madurai Kamraj University.

[65] Solaiyappan, Annamalai; Jayakrishnan, Jothi; Velmani, Sethu, (2011), Quality Measurement for hospital Services, 3rd International Conference on Information and Financial Engineering, IPERD, *12* (2011), pp. 246-250.

[66] Somnath Chatterjee (2015). A Study of Healthcare Management System in West Bengal With Special Reference to The District of Burdwan, University of Burdwan, Burdwan.

[67] Srinivasa Rao (2011), Marketing of Hospital Services, Published Thesis, Acharya Nagarjuna University.

[68] Sritharan, V, (2014), "Measuring Service Quality Dimensions: an Empirical Study of Private Hospitals in Jaffna District, Sri Lanka". Journal of Marketing and Consumer Research, 3.

[69] Subramanyam, V (1997), "Quality of care at Community Hospitals", Economic and Political Weekly, XXXII (37), September, 1997, pp. 20-21.

[70] Sudha.S.R (2012) "Private &Public Partnership in Healthcare services in India" Southern Economist, December 15, 2012, pp. 42-46.

[71] Sundaravadivelu A. B. (2013) Service Quality Strategies of Medical Services - A study with reference to Private hospitals in Chennai, Published Ph.D thesis, University of Madras.

[72] Teamur Aghamolaei; Tasnim Eghba Eftekhaari; Shideh Rafati; Kobra Kahnouji; Shamsieh Ahangari; Mohammad Esmaeil Shahrzad; Ataollah Kahnouji & Seyedeh Hamideh Hoseini (2014) Service Quality assessment of a referral hospital in Southern Iran with SERVQUAL technique: Patients' Perspective, BMC Health Services Research, 2014, pp 14-32.

[73] Thomas and Richard K. (2002), 'Treating patients like Customers' Marketing Health services, Summer 2002, *23 (2)*, p. 38.

[74] V. Andal (2016), Customer Service Quality – Relationship and Satisfaction (CSQ – R&S) In Health Care and Hospital

Services in Chennai City, Published Thesis, SavitribaiPhule University, Pune.

[75] Yogesh Pai, P (2011). Gaurav Ravi, Factors affecting In-Patient Satisfaction in Hosptial– A case study.International conference on Technology and Business Management, March 2011 pp 28-30.

3

Service Quality – Theoretical Framework

3.1 Introduction

Satisfaction is a person's feelings of pleasure or disappointment that result from comparing a product's perceived performance (or outcome) with expectations. Service Quality has been defined as "the outcome of an evaluation process where the consumer compares his expectations with the service he has received" or the difference between expected service and perceived service. Parasuraman, Zeithaml, and Berry (1988) state that, "Service quality is an abstract and elusive construct because of three features unique to services: intangibility, heterogeneity, and inseparability of production and consumption". Services are different from goods (tangible products) in terms of how they are produced, consumed, andevaluated. First of all, consumers can judge or experience the quality of tangible goods such as a new set of hospitals and hospital equipment prior to purchasing those tangible products. However, they are notable to judge the quality of intangible service products such as acquiring the experience in a hospital, stadium, resort, hotel or amusement park. Secondly, services, especially those involving high labour are heterogeneous, their performance often varies from producer to producer, from customer to customer, and from day to day (Zeithaml, Parasuraman, & Berry, 1990). Lastly, production and consumption of most services are inseparable (Zeithamletal.,1990). In other words, quality of service is often seen during service delivery, usually in an interaction between the customer and the provider, rather than being engineered at the manufacturing plant, and delivered intact to the customer (Zeithaml et al., 1990).

According to Berry and Parasuraman (1991),"services are dominated by experience qualities, attributes that can be meaningfully evaluated only after purchase and during production-consumption". In addition, customers do not evaluate Service Quality solely on the outcome of a service. They also consider the process of the service delivered whenever the event is completed (Zeithaml et al., 1990). Perception describes the processes by which we select organize and interprets information inputs to create a meaningful picture of the world. Customers compare the perceived services with the expected services. If the perceived services fall below the expected services customers are disappointed. The customers will got satisfied if their perception is above their expectation

Services are intangible and customers are often present during the process. Therefore, physical environment can have an influence on the customer perception of Service Quality (Baker et al., 2002;

Parasuraman et al., 1988). Customers' satisfaction is a combination of their cognitive and affective response to service encounters. Service Quality is the overall evaluation of a firm's service delivery system. Service Quality is the managerial delivery of services while satisfaction is the customers' experiences with those services. Improved Service Quality will result in more customer satisfaction (Bitner et al., 1994; Cronin & Taylor, 1992). Customers assessment of the product or service, its demand, alternative services available in the market and information gathered from others help them to evaluate the product/service in comparison with other products or services. Cognitive evaluation through information search results in customer's affective responses in the form of satisfaction or dissatisfaction. In such an evaluation, if customers' expectations are met with respect to human, technical and tangible aspects of the service, they are more likely to feel satisfied with the product/ service.

3.2 Characteristics of Service

There are four main characteristics which differentiate service from tangible product are as follows:

a) **Intangibility**: Tangible products are physically touchable, and the evaluation and perceptions of the customers can be done easily and effectively. On the contrary, services cannot be touched and can only be felt and consumed. The real challenges of the service marketing lie in this vital aspect.

b) **Inseparability**: Service cannot be separated from the actual situation to other or from service people to customers. The success of aservice organization lies with the person who delivers the service and the time of the delivery. Satisfaction may differ according to time, people and place involved.

c) **Perishability**: Services are not long-lasting and they will perish soon. The exact moment of the service is the heart of each service-centric business. This phenomenon is helpful to the

Sources: https://marketing-insider.eu/characteristics-of-services/

Figure 3.1 Characteristics of Service

industry in various aspects. Customers hardly get time to compare the previous services or to evaluate the present services at a go. As long as times are moving, the conceptualization of the situation gets risky to the customers.

d) **Inconsistency**: The Quality of Serviceschanges from time to time and place to place. It even gives a different quality of service for a person from the same organization within the change of short span of time. It also varies from people to people and it is a very difficult task to be consistent in service delivery.

3.3 Marketing Mix of Service Marketing

As far as service marketing is concerned, it adds three more mixes namely, process, people and physical evidence. In the preview of Hospital services as a whole, and the hospital sector, in particular, the seven marketing mixes observed are discussed below:

a) **Product**: It includes all ingredients or components assembled for the development of a given product. It also comprises the features, name of the brand or the organization especially in Hospitalscenario, and it also covers all services provided by the hospitals and the policy of the hospitalsand the quality of their services.

b) **Price**: It is nothing but the price of the product or services provided by hospitals. It also consists all payments made in relation to treatment. Satisfaction of the patients is directly related with cost of treatment.

c) **Promotion**: Advertising of the hospital services and their promotion activities are main dimensions under the promotion. Publicity of the hospitals and relations to the public also count under promotion mix.

d) **Place:** As far as the medical sectors are concerned, the place of service is very important. The areascovered and the distribution channel they followed matter very high. The tangible location of the hospitals contributes a lot. The place mix plays a vital role in the success of hospitals

f) **People**: The people are the most important mix in service marketing as the delivery of each service is directly connected with them. In goods or products, the people are away from the origin, i.e, factory and the chances of interaction are hidden. But in service, the service people have to interact directly with customers and the real momentum happens then. The positives and negatives are evaluated in real time, and the feedbacks are more strong and significant. More precisely, service encounters determine the success of a particular service.

g) **Physical Evidence:** Physical evidence is the tangible side of the services. As far as hospitals are concerned, the dominant physical evidence is the infrastructure, cleanliness, equipments, interiors inside the building and the parking facilities. The peripheral side of the physical evidence is less visible but it accounts greatly.

3.4 Types of Service Quality

The quality of service is usually measured in two dimensions, technical and functional. Technical quality is defined primarily on the basis of the technical accuracy of the activities and procedures. Several techniques for measuring technical quality have been proposed and are currently in use in various service organisations.Functional quality relates to the manner of delivery of various services. The total Service Quality can be subdivided as Basic Service Quality(BSQ), Value Added Service Quality (VASQ), and Critical Service Quality (CSQ).

3.4.1 Basic Service Quality (BSQ)

Though efforts have been made to study Basic Service Quality, there has been no general agreement on the measurement of the concept. The majority of the work to date has attempted to use the basic Service Quality of Parasuram's methodology in an effort to measure Service Quality. The SERVQUAL model of

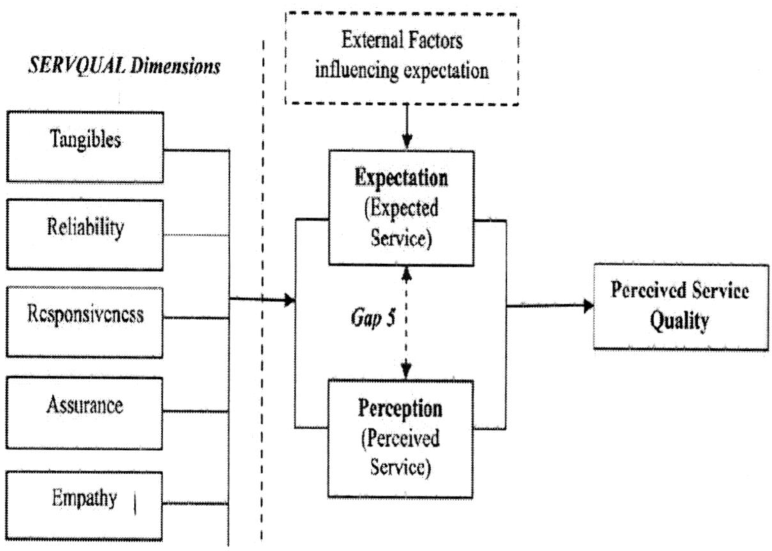

Source: Adapted from Zeithaml and Parasuraman (1988).

Figure 3.2 Basic Service Quality (BSQ) Model

Parasuram defined Service Quality gap in five dimensions These five dimensions enclose all the attributes of the Service Quality gap. The mentioned dimensions are as follows (Parasuraman et al., 1998):

- **Tangibles:** Physical facilities, equipment, and appearance of personnel.
- **Reliability:** Ability to perform the promised service dependably and accurately.
- **Responsiveness:** Willingness to help customers and provide prompt service.
- **Assurance:** Knowledge and courtesy of employees and their ability to inspire trust and confidence.
- **Empathy:** Caring, individualized attention the firm provides for its customers.

Based on the above basic dimensions, the dimension of basic Service Quality of hospitals and items in each dimension can be listed as follows

Table 3.1 List of variables in Basic Service Quality

Basic Service Quality	*Items in each Dimension*
Tangibility	Modern Equipment
	Visually appealing facilities
	Professional appearance
	Visually appealing materials
	Informative brochure
	Privacy during treatment
Reliability	Providing services as promised
	Maintaining error- free records
	Right at the first time itself
	Consistency of service
Responsiveness	Offers prompt services to patients
	Willingness to help patients

	Responsive doctors/ nurses
	Building confidence on patients
	Lesser waiting time
Assurance	Ability to handle patients problems
	Ability to instil confidence in patients
	Courteous behaviour at all times
	Knowledgeable staff
Empathy	Giving individual attention
	Dealings in a caring fashion
	Convenient consultation hours
	Obtaining feedback from patients

Basic Service Quality Model

3.4.2 Value Added Service Quality (VASQ)

Seven total quality health care dimensions have been included to measure the value added Service Quality of hospitals. The variables used to measure the Value Added Service Quality of hospitals are presented in the table below:

Table 3.2 List of variables in Value Added Service Quality (VASQ) in Hospitals

Value Added Service Quality	*Items in each Dimensions*
Infrastructure	Pre - and post- operative rooms
	Fresh and hygienic food
	Proper beds and resident rooms
	Availability of ambulance facility
	Diagnostic facility
	Availability of drug and blood
Personnel Quality	Competent doctors and nurses
	Adequate number of doctors and nurses
	Sincerity and regularity of all medical staff
	Frequency of discussion with patients
	Degree of teamwork among medical staff
	Personal attention by the medical staff

Process of clinical care	Investigation and examination by doctors
	Process of medical treatment by medical team
	Management of post-operative treatment
Administrative Procedure	Prompt and proper admission processes
	Access to emergency service care
	Acceptance of medico-legal cases
	Waiting time
	Getting appointment of specialists
Social responsibility	Fair medical treatment
	Good service at reasonable cost
	Conformity to ethical principles
	Assured privacy and confidentiality
	Free medical services to the needy patients
	Lesser consideration of economic indicators
Administrative Process	Reasonable waiting for all medical activities
	No delay or cancellation in scheduled treatment
	Provision of right patient services
	Seeking feedback and complaints
	Admission, stay and discharge process

3.4.3 Critical Service Quality in Health Care

Variables Related to Critical Service Quality are given in the following Table

Table 3.3: Variables Related to Critical Service

CSQ Variables	*Items in each Dimensions*
Personnel factors	Nurse's Behaviour
	Doctor's Behaviour
	Support Staff's Behaviour
	Inter Relationship Between Medical Staff
Operation Facilities Factor	Proper Scheduling
	Proper maintenance of operation system
	Adequate Equipment
Material Resource Factor	Proper Layout
	Adequate Consulting Hours
	Adequate Drugs

	Proper Communication Infrastructure
	Adequate pre-hospital services
Treatment Factor	Admission/ discharge protocol Organized daily rounds Antibiotic protocol Review
Communication Factor	Communication among doctors and patients Communication among nurses and patients Communication among Para-medical staff and patients IT-based communication
Acute Care Factor	Patient care regarding accident and emergency Patient care regarding operating works Patient care regarding intensive care units
	Patient care regarding dialysis

3.5 Quality of Services

Quality of goods and services is accepted as an important factor that determines the demand for goods and services. The competitive advantage of firms also depends on the quality of their outputs. Service Quality has been revealed as a key factor in the search for sustainable competitive advantage, differentiation and excellence in the service sector. Besides, it has been recognized as highly important for satisfying and retaining customers

The term 'quality' in the service sector seems to be different from the term in the goods market. The quality of a commodity can be evaluated and expressed in absolute terms, but it is not possible in the case of the service sector. Measurement of Service Quality is usually done with the help of Service Quality models (SERVQUAL MODELS).

3.6 Measuring Service Quality

Measuring Service Quality may involve both subjective and objective processes. In both cases, it is often some aspect of customer satisfaction which is being assessed. The most important and most used method to measure subjective elements of Service Quality is the SERVQUAL method. Objective processes may be subdivided into primary processes and

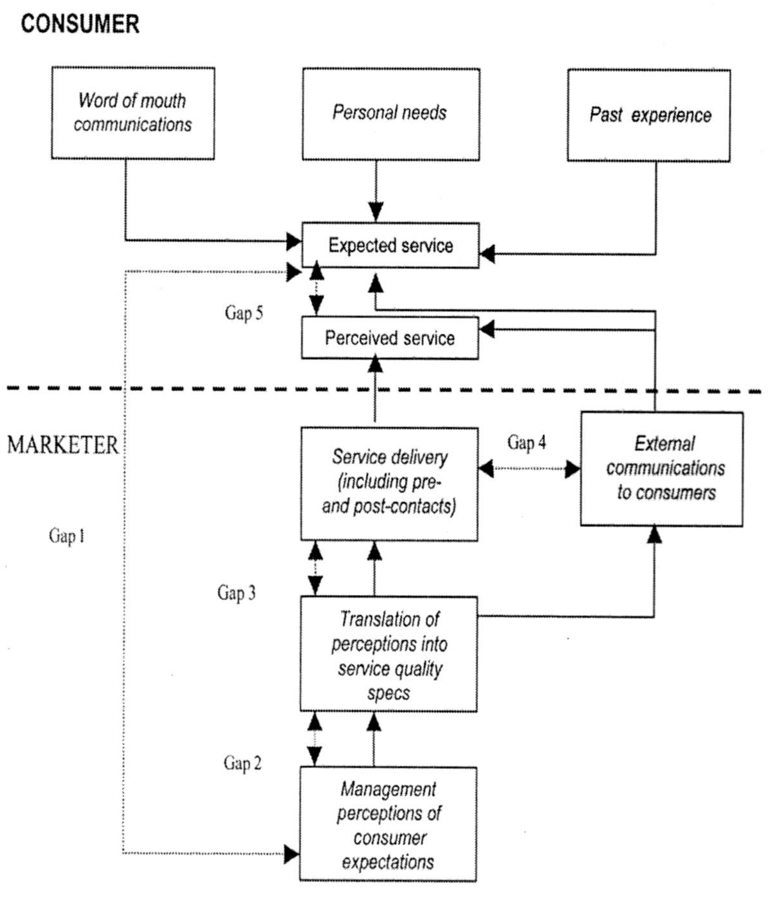

Source: Parasuraman et al. (1985)

Figure 3.3 The Gap Analysis Model

secondary processes. During primary processes, silent customers create test episodes of service, or the service episodes of normal customers are observed. In secondary processes, quantifiable factors such as numbers of customer complaints or numbers of returned goods are analysed in order to make inferences about Service Quality.

3.7 Service Quality Model

Customers generally have a tendency to compare the service they 'experience' with the service they 'expect'. If the experience does not match the expectation, there arises a gap.The Service Quality model or the 'GAP model' developed by a group of authors- Parasuraman, Zeithaml and Berry at Texas and North Carolina in 1985, highlights the main requirements for delivering high Service Quality. It identifies five 'gaps' that cause unsuccessful delivery. This model shows an integrated view of the consumer-company relationship.

The main idea of the model is focused on the assumption that service quality is dependent on the size and direction of the five gaps that can exist in the service delivery process.

3.8 Service Gaps (FIVE GAPS)

1.) *Gap between customer expectations and management perception:* It is the gap between customer expectations and those perceived by service provider to meet the customer's expectations.

2.) *Gap between management perception and Service Quality specifications:* It is the gap between management's perception of consumer expectations and the firm's Service Quality specifications.

3.) ***The gap between Service Quality specifications and service delivery.*** It arises due to the inefficiency, incapability or unwillingness from the part of the personnel who delivers the service.

4.) ***Gap between service delivery and external communication.*** This is the gap due tothe problems in the communication process. Statements made by company representatives and ads will affect customer expectation. This gap occurs if the actual services are not according to the statements,.

5.) ***Gap between perceived service and expected service.*** This gap occurs when the consumers misperceives the Service Quality.

3.9 Concept of Service Loyalty

Service loyalty is the degree to which a customer exhibits repeat purchasing behaviour from a service provider. They possess a positive attitudinal disposition toward the provider, and consider using only this provider when a need for this service arises.

3.9.1 Loyalty business model

The loyalty business model is a business model used in Strategic Management in which company resources are employed so as to increase the loyalty of customers and other stakeholders in the expectation that corporate objectives will be met or surpassed. A typical example of this type of model is quality of product or services leads to customer satisfaction, which leads to customer loyalty, which leads to profitability.

A model by Kaj Storbacka, Tore Strandvik, and Christian Grönroos (1994), called the Service Quality model, is more detailed than the basic loyalty business model but arrives at the same conclusion. In it, customer satisfaction is first based on a recent experience of the product or service. This assessment depends on prior expectations of overall quality compared to the actual performance received. If the recent experience exceeds prior expectations, customer satisfaction is likely to be high. This model then looks at the strength of the business relationship; it proposes that this strength is determined by the level of satisfaction with recent experience, overall perceptions of quality, customer commitment to the relationship, and bonds between the parties. This model then examines the link between relationship strength and customer loyalty. Customer loyalty is determined by three factors: relationship strength, perceived alternatives and critical episodes. The relationship can terminate if

1) the customer moves away from the company's service area,
2) the customer no longer has a need for the company's products or services,
3) more suitable alternative providers become available,
4) the relationship strength has weakened,
5) the company handles a critical episode poorly,

6) unexplainable change of price of the service provided.

The final link in the model is the effect of customer loyalty on profitability. The fundamental assumption of all the loyalty models is that keeping existing customers is less expensive than acquiring new ones. It is claimed byReichheld and Sasser (1990) that a 5 percent improvement in customer retention can cause an increase in profitability between 25 percent and 85 percent (in terms of NPV) depending upon the industry. However, Carrol and Reichheld (1992) dispute these calculations, claiming that they result from faulty cross-sectional analysis.

Loyalty can be defined as customers' continuing to believe that one organisation's product/service offer remains their best option. Customer loyalty is a deeply held commitment to repurchase a product/service consistently in the future despite some alternatives available in the market. *Moreover, loyalty means hanging in there even when there may be a problem because the organization has been good to them in the past and addresses issues when they arise. It means that they do not seek out competitors and, when approached by competitors, are not interested. It also means being willing to spend the time and effort to communicate with the organization so as to build on past successes and overcome any weaknesses.*The cost of attracting new customers is more than the cost of retaining old customers. Loyal customers have an emotional attachment with product/ service, and they cannot be attracted by any other brand that offers even a better deal.

Customer loyalty consists in attitudinal and behavioural loyalty. Attitudinal loyalty is customers' favourable inclination towards a product or service based on the cumulative experience. If an alternative brand with better attributes and a cheaper price is available in the market, such customers are likely to defect. On the contrary, behavioural loyalty is a strong commitment of customers to purchase the product/ service despite the availability of alternatives in the market. It represents the actual purchase behaviour of customers. It is also revealed through the willingness of customers to recommend that product/service to others. Loyal customers desire to continue the relationship with the firm. Repeat purchases and recommendations to other customers are indicators of loyalty.

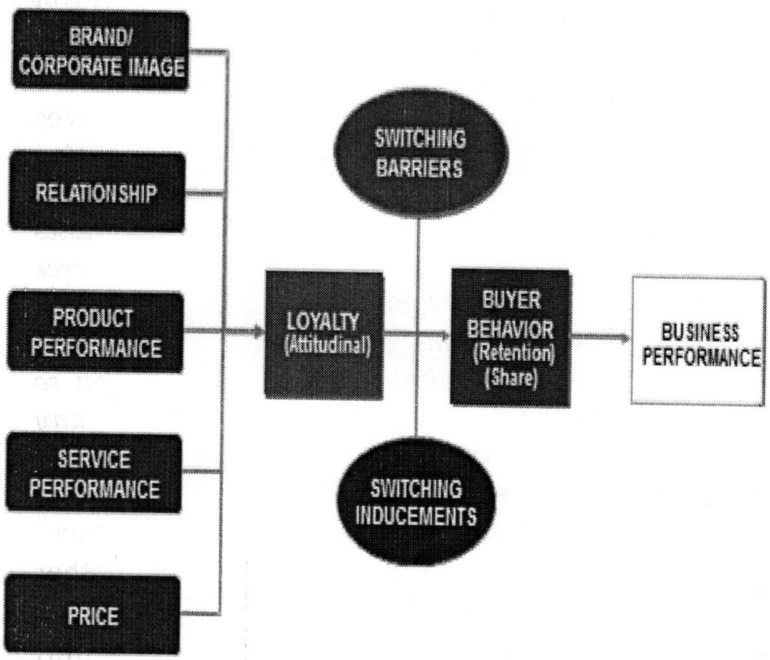

Figure 3.4 Customer Loyalty Conceptual Model

3.10 Expanded Models

Schlesinger and Heskett (1991) added employee loyalty to the basic customer loyalty model. They developed the concepts of "cycle of success" and "cycle of failure". In the cycle of success, ability to provide superior service to customers can be seen as a virtuous circle. Effort spent in selecting and training employees and creating a corporate culture in which they are empowered can lead to increased employee satisfaction and employee competence. This will likely to result in superior service delivery and customer satisfaction. This in turn will create customer loyalty, improved sales levels, and higher profit margins. Some of these profits can be reinvested in employee development thereby initiating another iteration of a virtuous cycle.

Figure 3.5 Virtuous Circle

3.11 History of Hospital

A hospital is a health care institution providing patient treatment with specialized staff and equipments. The best-known type of hospital is general hospital, which has an emergency department. Specialized hospitals include trauma centres, rehabilitation hospitals, children's hospitals, geriatric hospitals (seniors') and hospitals for dealing with specific medical needs such as psychiatric problems and certain disease categories. In the mid 19thcentury, hospitals and the medical profession became more professionalised, with a reorganisation of hospital management along more bureaucratic and administrative lines. The Apothecaries Act 1815 made it compulsory for medical students to practice for at least half a year at a hospital as part of their training. The Middle Ages saw the beginnings of support for hospital-like institutions by secular authorities.

The first recorded doctor's prescription came from Sumer in ancient Babylon under the rule of the dynasty of Hammurabi (1728-1686 BC). The Hammurabi code of law provides the first record of the regulation of doctors' practice, as well as the regulation of their fees. The Mesopotamian civilization made political, educational and medical contributions to the later development of the Egyptian, Hebrew, Persian and even Indian culture. Historical records show that efficient hospitals were constructed in India by 600 BC. During the splendid reign of King Asoka (273-232BC), Indian Hospitals started to look like modern hospitals. They followed principles of sanitation and caesarean sections were performed with close attention to technique in order to save both mother and child.

Physicians were appointed-one for every ten villages-to serve the health care needs of the populations and regional hospitals for the infirm and destitute were built by the Buddha. The first prominent Islamic hospital was founded in Damascus (Syria) in around 707 AD. However, most agree that the establishment at Baghdad was the most influential. The public hospital in Baghdad was opened during the Abbasid Caliphate of Harun-al-Rashid in the 8th century.

3.12 History of Hospital in India

In India, the health care systems are experiencing dramatic changes from what it was a few years ago. Health is a basic fundamental right of all citizens and health promotion forms an intrinsic part of health care. According to the World Health Organization, "health is a state of complete physical, social and mental wellbeing and not merely an absence of disease or infirmity." Since independence India had achieved remarkable progress in social political and economic fields. In the area of medical science too, commendable progress has been made during this period. However, unfortunately, hospital administration has lagged far behind. Even the most sophisticated and the so called modern hospitals in India continue to be governed by the stereotyped system of hospital administration, appointing the seniormost doctors as the focal points of education for the health professional and clinical research necessary for advancement of medicine. Thus the hospital is one of the most complex form of all administrative organizations (Directory of Hospitals, 1998).

Over the years, India has experienced a significant increase in the number of hospital beds to meet the growing health demands of its population. Hospitals as organizations face a number of challenges as they are exposed to greater risk compared to other industry, primarily because of the complexity of its operation, ensuring appropriate quality of care, humanitarian issues and various ethical dimensions facing health care (Government of India, 2003). Hospital is an economic institution with a significant social role in the community. It is not possible to discuss problems in medical and health care intelligently without reference to hospitals in terms of what they are, what they do, and how they do it. Hospitals in India have been organized on the British lines with strict hierarchical structure.

3.13 History of Hospitals in Kerala

Kerala has a long history of organized health care. Before the advent of European medicine, families of practitioners of indigenous system like Ayurveda handed their traditions from generation to generation. People were accustomed to approaching caregivers when they were sick, rather than turning to self-treatment. When the colonial powers established their presence in the region, they broughttheir medical system with them (Ramankutty, 2000). In 1900 as perthe direction of Maharaja of Travancore, a hospital was started at Neyyatinkara, which was considered as the first government hospital in Kerala. After this, many hospitals came up in South Travancore, Central Travancore and Malabar regions under the public Health system. As such, the public health system of Kerala has a glorious traditions of hundred and seven years. But actually the public health system strengthened only after the formation of united Kerala.

After 1957, for about 25 years, the graph of the public health system in Kerala shot up. However, there were some shortfalls in the sector during the last twenty-five years. (Gangadharan, 2007).

Health Sector Development in Kerala Kerala's healthcare system has garnered international acclaim. The state has a very good medical facility. The United Nations Children's Fund (UNICEF) and the World Health Organization designated Kerala the world's first "baby-friendly state" because of its effective promotion of breastfeeding over formulas. For example, more than 95 percentage of Keralite births are hospital-delivered. Aside from Ayurveda, Siddha, and Unani, many endangered and endemic modes of traditional medicine, including Kalari, Marmachikitsa, and Vishavaidyam, are practiced. These propagate via gurukula discipline and comprise a fusion of bothmedical and supernatural treatments, and are partly responsible for drawing increasing numbers of medical tourists. Kerala's remarkable achievements in health care were to a large extend based on its vast network of public health institutions which enabled her to earn the fame of "Kerala Model of Health" worth emulating even by advanced countries. The hallmark of this model was the low cost of health care, universal accessibility and availability to the poor sections of the society. This health model was made possible by many socio-economic conditions, important among which was the high female literacy rate in the state. Apart from these, the extensive network of medical institutions in modern medicine has also made this possible. Despite all these, Kerala faced some major problems in the health sector at the beginning of the 21st century. Difficult access to health care owing to high out of pocket health care expenditure has resulted in the impoverishment of a sizeable segment of the population. A major programme of the state in the11th plan has been to strengthen the public health system and provide universal health security (Economic Review,2010).

3.14 Types of Hospital

Some patients go to a hospital just for diagnosis, treatment or therapy and then leave (outpatients) without staying overnight, while others are admitted and stay overnight or for several days or weeks or months (inpatients'). Hospitals usually are distinguished from other types of medical facilities by their ability to admit and care for inpatients while the others often are described as clinics.

Further division can be on the basis of nature of hospitals:

1) **General Hospital** The best-known type of hospital is the general hospital, which is set up to deal with many kinds of disease and injury, and normally has an emergency department to deal with immediate and urgent threats to health.

2) **District Hospital:** A district hospital ,typically, is the major health care facility in its region, with large numbers of beds for intensive care and long-term care and specialized facilities for surgery, plastic surgery, childbirth, biopsy laboratories and so forth.

3) **Specialised Hospital**: This may include Super Speciality and Multi-Speciality hospitals. Types

of specialized hospitals include trauma centres, rehabilitation hospitals, children's hospitals, seniors' (geriatric) hospitals and hospitals for dealing with specific medical needs such as psychiatric problems (see psychiatric hospital), certain disease categories such as cardiac, oncological or orthopaedic problems and so forth.

4) **Teaching Hospital or Medical Colleges**: A teaching hospital combines assistance to patients with teaching to medical students and nurses and often is linked to a medical school, nursing school or university.

5) **Clinics**: A medical facility smaller than a hospital is generally called a clinic and is often run by a government agency for health services or a private partnership of physicians. Clinics generally provide only outpatient services.

3.15 Types of Treatment

3.15.1 Primary Care

Primary care is the term for the health care services which play a role in the local community. It refers to the work of health care professionals who act as a first point of consultation for all patients within the health care system. Such a professional would usually be a primary care physician such as a general practitioner or family physician, or a non-physician primary care provider. The common chronic illnesses usually treated in primary care units may include, for example: hypertension, diabetes, asthma, depression and anxiety& back pain. Primary care also includes many basic maternal and child health care services, such as family planning services and vaccinations.

3.15.2 Secondary Care

Secondary care comprises the health care services provided by medical specialists and other health professionals who generally do not have the first contact with patients, for example, cardiologists, urologists and dermatologists.

3.15.3 Tertiary Care

Tertiary care is specialized conductive health care usually for patients, and on referral from a primary or secondary health professional, a facility that has personnel and facilities for advanced medical investigation and treatment such as a tertiary referral hospital. Examples of tertiary care services are cancer management, neurosurgery, cardiac surgery, plastic surgery, treatment for severe burns, advanced neonatology services, palliative and other complex medical and surgical interventions.

3.15.4 Quaternary Care

The term 'quaternary care' is also used sometimes as an extension of tertiary care in reference to medicine of advanced levels which are highly specialized and not widely accessed. Experimental medicine and some types of uncommon diagnostic or surgical procedures are considered quaternary care. These services are usually only offered in a limited number of regional or national health care centres.

3.15.5 Home and Community Care

Many types of health care interventions are delivered outside of health facilities. They include many interventions of public health interest, such as food safety surveillance, distribution of condoms and needle exchange programmes for the prevention of transmissible diseases. They also include the services of professionals in residential and community settings in support of self-care, home care, long-term care, assisted living, treatment for substance use disorders, and other types of health and social care services.

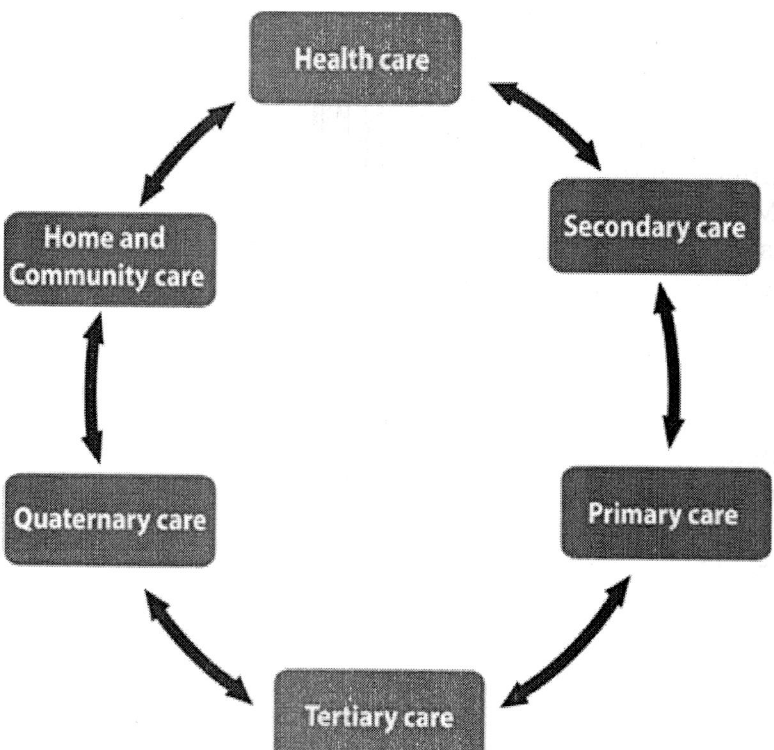

Figure 3.6 Types of Treatments

3.16 Quality in Health Care

Healthcare is a service that people need but do not necessarily want but, remarkably, healthcare is the fastest growing service in both developed and developing countries. The traditional services that once dominated the service sector-lodging, food service and house cleaning have been supplemented by modern banking, insurance, computing, communication and other business services. The interest in the measurement of Service Quality is understandably high in addition to the delivery of higher levels of a Service Quality strategy being suggested as critical to the service providers' efforts in positioning themselves more effectively in the marketplace (Yogesh et al., 2012). Service Quality has been revealed as a key factor in search for sustainable competitive advantage, differentiation and excellence in the service sector (Manish Joshi, 2014). Besides, it has been recognized as highly important forsatisfying and retaining customers.

3.17 Evolution of Quality in Health Care System

The fundamental goal of a health care system includes improving health outcome and responding to the legitimate expectations of the clients and health care providers. It requires adequate resources, which are not just financial, but also trained staff, appropriate facilities, equipment and pharmaceuticals. The movement of quality in health care began in the 1990s. In the US, the modern quality assurance movement in health care began in 1917. Improving quality care over the years evolved from quality control to quality assurance, and this in turn evolved to total quality management. Recently the latter has evolved to population health improvement (WHO, 2000).

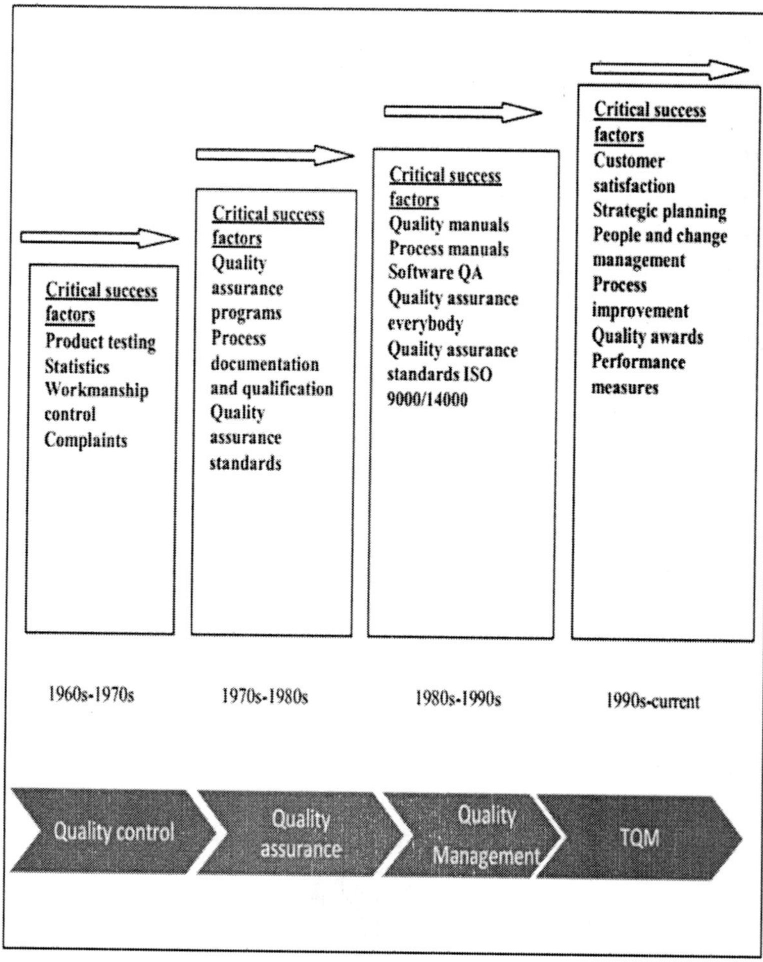

Source www.google.com

Figure 3.7 Quality Testing

3.18 Dimensions of Service Quality

Quality is a comprehensive and multifaceted concept. Experts generally recognizeseveral distinct dimensions of quality that vary in importance depending on thecontext in which a Quality Assurance effort takes place. QA activities may address one or more dimensions, such as technical competence, access to services, effectiveness, interpersonal relations, efficiency, continuity, safety, and amenities. These dimensions of quality are a useful framework that helps health teams to define and analyse their problems and to measure the extent to which they are meeting program standards. The eight dimensions discussed in detail in this section have been developed from the technical literature on quality, and synthesize ideas from various QA experts. These dimensions of quality are as appropriate for clinical care as for management services that support service delivery.

1. **Technical Competence**: Technical competence includes the skills, capabilities & actual performance of health providers and supporting staff. Technical competence related with how well health care providers execute practice guidelines and all standards in terms of accuracy, reliability and consistency. These are relevant for all type of clinical care related to prevention, diagnosis, treatment and health counselling. Technical competency is also related with material resources. For example: an X-ray machine must produce radiation and meet standards. A lack of competency reduces effectiveness and also endangers patient safety or security.

2. **Access to Services:** Access is connected to approachability, which meansthat the operating hours are convenient, the location of the facilities

are convenient, the waiting times are short and also easy access through telephone. Access means that health care services are totally unrestricted by geographic, economic, social, cultural, organizational or linguistic barriers. Geographic access may be measured by modes of transportation, distance, travel time and any other physical barriers that could keep the client from receiving care. Economic access refers to the affordability of products and services for clients. Social or cultural access relates to service acceptability within the context of the client's cultural values, beliefs, and attitudes. For example, family planning services are usually not accepted when they are consistent with the local culture. Organisational access refers to the extent to which services are conveniently organized for prospective clients and encompasses issues such as clinic hours and appointment systems, waiting time and the mode of service delivery.

3. **Effectiveness:** Effectiveness is measured in terms ofhowthe firm is ableto meet the desired level of outcomes and the pre-established goals. Thequality of health services depends on the effectiveness of service deliverynorms and clinical guidelines.

4. **Interpersonal Relations**: It means keeping the customer informed in away they can understand and also listen to the patients about specific requirements providing individualised attention and also recognizing regular patients. The dimension of interpersonal relations refers to

the interaction between providers and clients, managers and health care providers, and the health team and the community. Good interpersonal relations establish trustand credibility through demonstrations of respect, confidentiality, courtesy, responsiveness, and empathy. Effective listening and communication are also important. Sound interpersonal relations contribute to effective health counselling and to a positive rapport with patients. Inadequate interpersonal relations can reduce the effectiveness of a technically competent healthservice.

5. **Efficiency:** The efficiency of health services is an important dimension ofquality because it affects product and service affordability and because healthcare resources are usually limited. Efficient services provide optimal rather than maximum care to the patient and the community; they provide the greatest benefit within the reasonable resources available. Efficiency demands that necessary or appropriate care is provided. Poor care resulting from ineffective norms or incorrect delivery should be minimized or eliminated. In this way, quality can be improved and it also helps in reducing costs. Harmful care, besides causing unnecessary risk and patient discomfort, is often expensive and time-consuming to correct and it would be misleading too,however, toimply that quality improvements never require additional resources. But by analysing efficiency, health program managers may select the most cost effective intervention.

6. **Continuity:** Continuity means that the client receives the complete range of health services that he or she needs, without interruption or unnecessary repetition of diagnosis or treatment. Services must be offered on an ongoing basis. The client must have access to routine and preventive care provided by ahealth worker who knows his or her medical history. A client must also have access to timely referral for specialized services and to complete follow- upcare.
7. **Safety:** Safety means freedom from danger, risk or doubts. It includes physical safety, financial security and confidentiality. As a dimension ofquality, safety means minimizing the risks of injury, infection, harmful side-effects, or other dangers related to service delivery. Safety involves the provider as well as the patient. For example, safety is an important dimension of quality for blood transfusions, especially since the advent of AIDS. Patients must be protected from infection, and health workers who handle blood and needles must be protected by safety procedures. Additional safety issues related to blood transfusions include maintaining aseptic conditions and using proper techniques for transfusing blood. While safety may seem most important when complex clinical services are provided, there are safety concerns in the provision of basic health services as well.
8. **Amenities:** Amenities refer to the features of health services that do not directly relate to clinical effectiveness but may enhance the client's satisfaction and willingness to return

to the facility for subsequent health care needs. Amenities are also important because they may affect the client's expectations about, and confidence in, other aspects of the service or product. Where cost recovery is a consideration, amenities may enhance the client'swillingness to payfor services. Amenities relate to the physical appearance of facilities, personnel, and materials, as well as to comfort, cleanliness, and privacy. Other amenities may include features that make the waiting time more pleasant such as music, educational or recreational videos, and reading materials.

Service Quality is usually defined as the outcome of an evaluation process where the consumer compares his expectations with the service he has received or the difference between expected and obtained services. Competition between Hospitals in Kerala is growing day by day, as the competition increases quality of services is compromised. In the era of competition, Professional management of hospitals is becoming important in order to enhance efficiency and effectiveness of the services.In this chapter basic theories and concepts of Service Quality are discussed. In the study attempt has been made to analyse the service Quality of Hospitals in Kerala.

REFERENCES

[1] Ahenkan, A. &Aduo-Adjei, K. (2017), Predictors of Patient Satisfaction with Quality of Healthcare in University Hospitals in Ghana, Hospital Practices and Research, *2*(1): pp. 9-14.

[2] Ahmed, S. Tarique, K.M. &Arif, I. (2017),"Service quality, patient satisfaction and loyalty in the Bangladesh healthcare sector", International Journal of health care quality assurance, *30*(5): pp477-488.

[3] Aiello A., Garman A. & Morris B.S. (2003),"Patient satisfaction with nursing care: A multilevel analysis", Journal of Quality Management in Health Care, *12*(3): pp. 187-191.

[4] Ajam, M., Sadeghifar, J., Anjomshoa, M., Mahmoudi, S., Honarvar, H. &Mousavi, S. M. (2014),"Assessing quality of healthcare service by the SERVQUAL model: A case study of a field hospital", Journal of Military Medicine, *15*(4): pp. 273–279.

[5] Ajarmah, B.S. & Hashem, T.N. (2015),"Patient Satisfaction evaluation on Hospitals; Comparison Study between accredited and non accredited hospitals in Jordan", European Scientific Journal, *11*(32): pp. 298-314.

[6] Akbar, F.H. & Jaya, M.T. (2017),"Relationship between Service Quality on Public Health Center and Patient Satisfaction", Global Journal of Health Science, *9*(7): pp. 96-102.

[7] Amira Elleuch (2005), "Patient Satisfaction in Japan", International Journal of Health Care Quality Assurance, *21* (7), 2005.

[8] Boshoff, C. and Gray, B., (2001) "The relationship between Service Quality, Customer Satisfaction and Buying Intentions in the Private Hospital Industry", South African Journal of Business Management, pp. 35.

[9] Bowers, M.R., Swan, J.E., and Koehler, W., (1994) "What Attributes Determine Quality and Satisfaction with Health Care Delivery?", Health Care Management Review, *19* (4).

[10] Brown, S.W. and Swartz, T.W.,(1989) "A Gap Analysis of Professional Service Quality", Journal of Marketing, *53* (4).

[11] Choi, K.S., Lee, H., Kein, C. and Lee, S., (2005), "The Service Quality Dimensions and Patient Satisfaction Relationship in South Korea: Comparison Across Gender, Age and Type of Service", The Journal of Service Marketing, *19*(3), 2005.

[12] Ali, S.S. & Ahmed, F. (2010): "Measuring Indian Patients' Satisfaction: a case of Private Hospitals", Portuguese Journal of Management Studies, *15*(3) pp. 303-329.

[13] Ali, S.S. Kaur, R. Pande, M.J.C. and Ahmad, F. (2014): "Service quality gap approach: A case of Indian customer's satisfaction of private banks", International Journal of Business Excellence, *7* (4): 429–453.

[14] Alijanzadeh, M. Moosaniaye Zare, S. A. Rajaee, R. Mohammad Ali M.F.S. Asefzadeh, S. Alijanzadeh, M. & Gholami, S. (2016): Comparison Quality of Health Services between Public and Private Providers: The Iranian People's Perspective, Electron Physician, *8*(9).

[15] Aliman, N.K. &Mohamad, W.N. (2016): Linking Service Quality, Patients' Satisfaction and Behavioral Intentions: An investigation on Private Healthcare in Malaysia, Procedia - Social and Behavioral Sciences, *224*(2016): pp. 141–148.

[16] Coddington, D., Fischer, E., Moore, K., and Clarke, R. (2007), "Beyond Managed Care–How Consumers and Technology are Changing the future of Health Care", Jossey-Bass, San Francisco, CA, 2007.

[17] David Camilleri and Mark O'Callaghan,(2003) "Comparing Public and Private Hospital Care Service Quality", International Journal of Health Care Quality, *11*(4).

[18] Devabakan, N., and Akgarayli, M.(2012), "The Usage of SERVQUAL scores for the Measurement of Quality of Perceived Service in Health Facilities and Implementation of Private Altimordu Hospital", Journal of Institute of Social Sciences, *5* (1).

[19] Dursun, Y. and Cerci, M. (2012), "Perceived Service Quality: A Study on Patient Satisfaction and Behavioural Factors", Journal of Community Health, *24*(1).

[20] Gooding, S.K.S., (1995), "Quality, Sacrifice and Value in Hospital Choice", Journal of Health Care Marketing, *15* (4).

[21] Grandzol, J.R., and Gershown, M., (2010), "Which TQM Practices Really Matter: An Empirical Investigation", Quality Measurement Journal, *4* (1).

[22] Hausman (2004), A., "Professional Service Relationship: A Multi Context Study of Factors Impacting Satisfaction,

Repatronization and Recommendation", The Journal of Service Marketing, *17*(2&3).

[23] Hwang, L., Eves, A. and Desombre, T., (2009) "Gap Analysis of Patient Meal Service Perceptions", International Journal of Health Care Quality Assurance, 16 (9), 2003. K. Vaidyanathan, "ESI Scheme a Waste, Fear Junior Executives", The Indian Express, *128*, p. 8.

[24] Kui-Son Choi, Hanjoon Lee, Chankon Kim and Suhbee Lee, (2002)"The Service Quality Dimensions and Patient Satisfaction Relationship in South Korea: Comparisons Across Agenda, Age and Types of Services", Journal of Services Marketing, *19* (3).

[25] Lam, S.S.K, (1997) "SERVQUAL: A Tool for Measuring Patients Opinions of Hospital Service Quality in Hong Kong", Total Quality Management, *8*(4).

4

Factors Affecting Service Quality in Government and Private Sector Hospitals in Kerala

A service is any act or performance that one party can offer to another, it is essentially intangible and does not result in the ownership of anything. Its production may or may not be tied to a physical output. The importance of the service sector is growing day by day. Service Industries are present in all sectors. We can find service organisations both in private and public sector. The Government sector has hospitals, loan agencies, military services, police and fire departments, post offices, regulatory agencies and schools. Services in the private non-profit sector include museums, charities, churches, colleges, foundations and hospitals. Airlines, banks, hotels, insurance firms, law firms, consulting firms medical practices and real estate firms comes under the service business. The traditional services include lodging, foodservice, and housecleaning etc. Today, they have been supplemented by super speciality hospitals, modern banking, insurance, computing, communication, and other business services. In modern days hospital industry is gaining importance as lifestyle diseases and other diseases are increasing. We can find large number of hospitals both in private and public sector.

Satisfaction is a person's feeling of pleasure or disappointment that result from comparing a product's perceived performance (or outcome) to expectations. Service Quality has been defined as "the outcome of an evaluation process where the consumer compares his expectations with the service he has received or the difference between expected service and perceived service. Parasuraman, Zeithaml, and Berry (1988) stated that," Service Quality is an abstract and elusive construct because of three features unique to services: intangibility, heterogeneity, and inseparability of production and consumption". Services are different from goods (tangible products) in terms of how they are produced, consumed, and evaluated.

This study attempts to have a look at the factors that influence the Service Quality. For this purpose, primary data were collected from a sample of 550 patients of government and private hospitals, by using a well-structured Interview Schedule. Various statements were used to identify the factors influencing patient satisfaction. Patients' satisfaction is commonly identified as the yardstick for the Service Quality of hospitals

This Chapter deals with the demographic profile of the selected patients with Frequency tables and Cross-tabulation. Various factors affecting the satisfaction and loyalty were analysed with the help of Discriminant Analysis, Freidman Test, Mann Whitney U Test and Kruskal Wallis Test. Step wise multiple Regression is applied to identify the factors affecting overall satisfaction level of patients. Multiple DiscriminantAnalysis is applied to discriminate the variables affecting the overall satisfaction of patients in relation to the Service Quality of both government and private hospitals.

4.1 Profile of Selected Patients

The primary data were collected from 550 patients. The following Table gives details about the demographic and occupational status of the selected patients.

Table 4.1 Profile of Selected patients

Sl.No.	*Category*	*No. of Repondents*	*Percentage*
1	Age		
	Below 20	96	17.5
	20-40	262	47.6
	41-60	72	13.1
	61-80	96	17.5
	Above 80	24	4.4
2.	Gender		
	Male	240	43.6
	Female	310	56.4
3.	Marital Status		
	Married	360	65.5
	Unmarried	118	21.5
	Widower	48	8.7
	Divorcee	24	4.4

4.	Educational Qualification		
	Upto SSLC	191	34.7
	Diploma	97	17.6
	Graduate	166	30.2
	Post Graduate	48	8.7
	Others	48	8.7
5.	Occupational Status		
	Self Employed	144	26.2
	Govt. Employee	121	22.0
	Private Employees	119	21.6
	Professional	72	13.1
	Others	94	17.1
6.	Annual Income		
	Less than 1,00,000	120	21.8
	1,00,000-2,00,000	192	34.9
	2,00,001-5,00,000	215	39.1
	5,00,001-10,00,000	23	4.2
7.	Area of Residence		
	Urban	215	39.1
	Semi Urban	168	30.5
	Rural	167	30.4
8.	Nature and Type of Hospitals		
	a. Government/Public Sector		
	Medical College	120	21.8
	District Hospitals	72	13.1
	Taluk Hospitals	48	8.7
	Primary Health Centre	24	4.4

	Others	48	8.7
	b. Private Hospitals		
	Medical Colleges	48	8.7
	Multi-Speciality	95	17.3
	Super-Speciality	95	17.3
9.	Area of hospitals		
	Urban	383	69.6
	Semi Urban	47	8.5
	Rural	120	21.8
10.	Category of Treatment		
	Surgical	263	47.8
	Medical	167	30.4
	Maternity	120	21.8
11.	Frequency of health checkup of		
	When there is a need	145	26.4
	Once in a week	142	25.8
	Twice in a month	216	39.3
	Once in a month	47	8.5
12.	Source of Information		
	Proximity to residence	48	8.7
	Medical professionals	145	26.4
	Friends	215	39.1
	Relatives	94	17.1
	Ex-patients	48	8.7

Source: Survey Data

From the above Table, it can be found that, out of the 550 selected patients 56.4 per cent were female and 43.6 per cent were male. Regarding age 47.6 per cent belong to the age group 20-40 and 4.4 per cent were above 80. Out ofthe 550 patients selected, 65.5 percent were married and 21.5 were unmarried and 8.7 percent were widower and4.4 percent were divorcee.

Regarding the educational status of respondents, 34.7 per cent had education up to SSLC, 17.6per cent are diploma holders 30.2per cent were graduates 8.7 per cent were post graduates and 8.7 per cent held other educational qualification. From the table it is clear that 26.2 per cent of the patients were self-employed and 22 per cent were Govt. Employees and 21.6 per cent were Private employees and 13.1per cent were professionals and 17.1 per cent were workers. Out of the patients selected 39.1 per cent were in the income group of 200001-500000 and 34.9 per cent were in the income group of 100000-200000. Out of the patients selected,39.10 per cent were from urban area, 30.5 per cent were from semi-urban areas and 30.4 per cent were from rural area.Out of the Patients selected 69.60 per cent prefer hospitals in the Urban areas and 8.5 per cent preferred Semi urban areas and 21.8 per cent preferred hospitals in the rural areas.

Regarding the type of hospitals 21.8per cent preferred Government Medical Colleges, and 13.1 per cent opted District Hospitals, 8.7 per cent preferred Taluk Hospitals, 4.4 per cent opted Primary Health and 8.7 per cent opted other health care facilities in the Government sector.8.7 per cent approached private medical colleges, 17.3 opted private Multi Speciality hospitals and again 17.3 per cent went for private Super speciality hospitals. Out of selected patients the largest number(47.80 per cent) visited hospitals for Surgical needs, 30.40 per cent approached for other medical needs, and 21.8 per cent visits for maternity purposes. Out of the patients selected, 39.1 per cent of the patients came to know about hospitals from their friends, whereas 26.40 per cent got information from medical professionals and 17.1 per cent came to know about hospitals from their relatives, and 8.7 per cent people get information fromEx – patients. Regarding the frequency of visits, 39.30per cent visited hospitals twice in a month and 26.4 per cent visited hospital when there was a need and 25.8 per cent visited hospitals once in a week and 8.5 per cent once in a month.

4.2 Gender wise Distribution

Gender wise Distribution of patients is presented in the following table.

Table 4.2 Nature and Type of Hospital* Gender

		Gender		*Total*
		Male	*Female*	
Government Hospitals				
Medical College	Count	48	72	120
	% within Nature and Type of Hospital	40.0%	60.0%	100.0%
District Hospital	Count	25	47	72
	% within Nature and Type of Hospital	34.7%	65.3%	100.0%
Taluk Hospital	Count	24	24	48
	% within Nature and Type of Hospital	50.0%	50.0%	100.0%
Primary Health Centre	Count	24	0	24
	% within Nature and Type of Hospital	100.0%	0.0%	100.0%
Others	Count	24	24	48
	% within Nature and Type of Hospital	50.0%	50.0%	100.0%

Private Hospitals				
Medical Colleges	Count	0	48	48
	% within Nature and Type of Hospital	0.0%	100.0%	100.0%
Multi speciality	Count	71	24	95
	% within Nature and Type of Hospital	74.7%	25.3%	100.0%
Super Speciality	Count	24	71	95
	% within Nature and Type of Hospital	25.3%	74.7%	100.0%
Total	Count	240	310	550
	% within Nature and Type of Hospital	43.6%	56.4%	100.0%

Source: Survey Data

From the table No. 4.2, it can be found that, out of the 550 selected patients, the majority, (56.4 per cent) were female and 43.6 per cent were male, 74.7 per cent patients in the private multi-speciality hospitals were male and 74.7 per cent patients in the private super speciality were female.

4.3 Age-wise Classification of Patients

From above Table it is clear that the largest numberof the respondents (47.6 per cent) belonged to the age group of 20-40 and 4.4 per cent were above 80. Out of the patients who opted government medical colleges, 40 per cent belonged to the age group 61-80. In the case of District hospitals, 100 per cent were in the age group of 20-40. In the case of Taluk hospitals 50 per cent of respondents were in the age group of 20-40 and 50 per cent were in the age group of 41-60. In the case of Primary health centre 100 per cent were above 80. In the case of Private medical colleges, 50 per cent hadage below 20 and 50 per cent werein the age group of 61-80.

The following table presents agewise distribution of selected patients among different types of hospitals.

Table 4.3 Nature and Type of Hospital * Age

			Age					Total
			Below 20	20-40	41-60	61-80	Above 80	
Government Hospitals	Medical College	Count	24	24	24	48	0	120
		% within Nature and Type of Hospital	20.0%	20.0%	20.0%	40.0%	0.0%	100.0%
	District Hospital	Count	0	72	0	0	0	72
		% within Nature and Type of Hospital	0.0%	100.0%	0.0%	0.0%	0.0%	100.0%
	Taluk Hospital	Count	0	24	24	0	0	48
		% within Nature and Type of Hospital	0.0%	50.0%	50.0%	0.0%	0.0%	100.0%
	Primary Health Centre	Count	0	0	0	0	24	24
		% within Nature and Type of Hospital	0.0%	0.0%	0.0%	0.0%	100.0%	100.0%
	Others	Count	0	48	0	0	0	48
		% within Nature and Type of Hospital	0.0%	100.0%	0.0%	0.0%	0.0%	100.0%
Private Hospitals	Medical Colleges	Count	24	0	0	24	0	48
		% within Nature and Type of Hospital	50.0%	0.0%	0.0%	50.0%	0.0%	100.0%
	Multi speciality	Count	24	47	24	0	0	95
		% within Nature and Type of Hospital	25.3%	49.5%	25.3%	0.0%	0.0%	100.0%
	Super Speciality	Count	24	47	0	24	0	95
		% within Nature and Type of Hospital	25.3%	49.5%	0.0%	25.3%	0.0%	100.0%
Total		Count	96	262	72	96	24	550
		% within Nature and Type of Hospital	17.5%	47.6%	13.1%	17.5%	4.4%	100.0%

Source: Survey Data.

Table 4.4 indicates the marital status of the selected patients

Table 4.4 Nature and Type of Hospital * Marital Status

			Marital Status				Total
			Married	Unmarried	Widower	Divorcee	
Government Hospitals	Medical College	Count	96	24	0	0	120
		% within Nature and Type of Hospital	80.0%	20.0%	0.0%	0.0%	100.0%
	District Hospital	Count	72	0	0	0	72
		% within Nature and Type of Hospital	100.0%	0.0%	0.0%	0.0%	100.0%
	Taluk Hospital	Count	24	24	0	0	48
		% within Nature and Type of Hospital	50.0%	50.0%	0.0%	0.0%	100.0%
	Primary Health Centre	Count	24	0	0	0	24
		% within Nature and Type of Hospital	100.0%	0.0%	0.0%	0.0%	100.0%
	Others	Count	48	0	0	0	48
		% within Nature and Type of Hospital	100.0%	0.0%	0.0%	0.0%	100.0%
Private Hospitals	Medical Colleges	Count	0	24	0	24	48
		% within Nature and Type of Hospital	0.0%	50.0%	0.0%	50.0%	100.0%
	Multi speciality	Count	24	23	48	0	95
		% within Nature and Type of Hospital	25.3%	24.2%	50.5%	0.0%	100.0%
	Super Speciality	Count	72	23	0	0	95
		% within Nature and Type of Hospital	75.8%	24.2%	0.0%	0.0%	100.0%
Total		Count	360	118	48	24	550
		% within Nature and Type of Hospital	65.5%	21.5%	8.7%	4.4%	100.0%

Source: Survey Data

The following Table represents the educational qualification of the selected patients.

Table 4.5 Nature and Type of Hospital * Educational Qualification

			Educational Qualification					Total
			Upto SSLC	Diploma	Graduation	Post Graduation	Others	
Government Hospitals	Medical College	Count	72	24	24	0	0	120
		% within Nature and Type of Hospital	60.0%	20.0%	20.0%	0.0%	0.0%	100.0%
	District Hospital	Count	47	25	0	0	0	72
		% within Nature and Type of Hospital	65.3%	34.7%	0.0%	0.0%	0.0%	100.0%
	Taluk Hospital	Count	0	0	24	0	24	48
		% within Nature and Type of Hospital	0.0%	0.0%	50.0%	0.0%	50.0%	100.0%
	Primary Health Centre	Count	24	0	0	0	0	24
		% within Nature and Type of Hospital	100.0%	0.0%	0.0%	0.0%	0.0%	100.0%
	Others	Count	0	24	0	24	0	48
		% within Nature and Type of Hospital	0.0%	50.0%	0.0%	50.0%	0.0%	100.0%
Private Hospitals	Medical Colleges	Count	24	0	0	24	0	48
		% within Nature and Type of Hospital	50.0%	0.0%	0.0%	50.0%	0.0%	100.0%
	Multi-speciality	Count	0	24	71	0	0	95
		% within Nature and Type of Hospital	0.0%	25.3%	74.7%	0.0%	0.0%	100.0%
	Super Speciality	Count	24	0	47	0	24	95
		% within Nature and Type of Hospital	25.3%	0.0%	49.5%	0.0%	25.3%	100.0%
Total		Count	191	97	166	48	48	550
		% within Nature and Type of Hospital	34.7%	17.6%	30.2%	8.7%	8.7%	100.0%

Source: Survey Data

4.4 Marital Status

From the table No. 4.4 we can see that, out of 550 patients selected 65.5 per cent were married and 21.5 were unmarried, 8.7 per cent were widower and 4.4 per cent were divorcees. Among those who opted Govt. medical colleges 80 per cent were married and 20 per cent were unmarried. Among the patients in Private medical colleges 50 per cent were unmarried and 50 per cent were divorcees. In the case of primary health centre 100 per cent were married.

4.5 Educational Qualification of Patients

From the above table it is clear that a large number of the respondents (34.7 per cent) had education up to SSLC, 17.6 per cent were diploma holders, 30.2 per cent are graduates 8.7 per cent were post graduates and 8.7 per cent held other educational qualification. Out of the patients who opted government medical colleges, 60 per cent have educational qualification up to SSLC. In the case of District hospitals 65.3 per cent were diploma holders. In the case of Taluk hospitals 50 per cent of respondents were graduates and 50 per cent held other degrees. In the case of Primary health centre 100 per cent hadeducational qualification up to SSLC. In the case of Private medical college 50 per cent had educational qualification up to SSLC and 50 per cent were Post Graduates.

The occupational status of the patients is described in the following table

Table 4.6 Nature and Type of Hospital * Occupational Status

			Occupational Status					Total
			Self Employed	Govt. Employee	Private Employee	Professional	Worker	
Government Hospitals	Medical College	Count	72	0	24	24	0	120
		% within Nature and Type of Hospital	60.0%	0.0%	20.0%	20.0%	0.0%	100.0%
	District Hospital	Count	24	25	0	0	23	72
		% within Nature and Type of Hospital	33.3%	34.7%	0.0%	0.0%	31.9%	100.0%
	Taluk Hospital	Count	0	24	0	0	24	48
		% within Nature and Type of Hospital	0.0%	50.0%	0.0%	0.0%	50.0%	100.0%
	Primary Health Centre	Count	0	0	0	0	24	24
		% within Nature and Type of Hospital	0.0%	0.0%	0.0%	0.0%	100.0%	100.0%
	Others	Count	0	24	0	24	0	48
		% within Nature and Type of Hospital	0.0%	50.0%	0.0%	50.0%	0.0%	100.0%
Private Hospitals	Medical Colleges	Count	0	24	0	24	0	48
		% within Nature and Type of Hospital	0.0%	50.0%	0.0%	50.0%	0.0%	100.0%
	Multi speciality	Count	0	0	95	0	0	95
		% within Nature and Type of Hospital	0.0%	0.0%	100.0%	0.0%	0.0%	100.0%
	Super Speciality	Count	48	24	0	0	23	95
		% within Nature and Type of Hospital	50.5%	25.3%	0.0%	0.0%	24.2%	100.0%
Total		Count	144	121	119	72	94	550
		% within Nature and Type of Hospital	26.2%	22.0%	21.6%	13.1%	17.1%	100.0%

Source: Survey Data

4.6 Occupational Status

From the table it is clear that 26.2 per cent of the patients are self-employed and 22 per cent were Govt. Employees and 21.6 per cent were Private employees and 13.1per cent are professional and 17.1per cent were workers. Among the patients who opted Govt. medical colleges 60 per cent were self-employed and in the case of those who opted private medical colleges, 50 per cent were Government employees and50 per cent were professionals.

4.7 Annual Income of Patients

Out of the patients selected, 39.1 per cent were in the group of 200001-500000, 34.9 per cent were in the income group of 100000-200000. Those who selected Govt. medical college, 40 per cent have income less than 100000 and of those who selected primary health centres 100 per cent had income less than 100000.

4.8 Area of Residence

From Table 4.8 it is clear that out of the patients selected,a large number (39.10 per cent) were from urban area and 30.5 were from semi urban area and 30.4 per cent were from rural area. Of those who selected private medical colleges 100 per cent were from Urban area

Table 4.7 represents Annual Income of the Patients

Table 4.7 Nature and Type of Hospital * Annual Income

			Annual income				Total
			Less than 100000	100000-200000	200001-500000	500001-1000000	
Government Hospitals	Medical College	Count	48	48	24	0	120
		% within Nature and Type of Hospital	40.0%	40.0%	20.0%	0.0%	100.0%
	District Hospital	Count	24	48	0	0	72
		% within Nature and Type of Hospital	33.3%	66.7%	0.0%	0.0%	100.0%
	Taluk Hospital	Count	0	48	0	0	48
		% within Nature and Type of Hospital	0.0%	100.0%	0.0%	0.0%	100.0%
	Primary Health Centre	Count	24	0	0	0	24
		% within Nature and Type of Hospital	100.0%	0.0%	0.0%	0.0%	100.0%
	Others	Count	0	24	24	0	48
		% within Nature and Type of Hospital	0.0%	50.0%	50.0%	0.0%	100.0%
Private Hospitals	Medical Colleges	Count	24	0	24	0	48
		% within Nature and Type of Hospital	50.0%	0.0%	50.0%	0.0%	100.0%
	Multi speciality	Count	0	0	95	0	95
		% within Nature and Type of Hospital	0.0%	0.0%	100.0%	0.0%	100.0%
	Super Speciality	Count	0	24	48	23	95
		% within Nature and Type of Hospital	0.0%	25.3%	50.5%	24.2%	100.0%
Total		Count	120	192	215	23	550
		% within Nature and Type of Hospital	21.8%	34.9%	39.1%	4.2%	100.0%

Source: Survey Data

Area of residence of patients is represented in the following table

Table 4.8 Nature and Type of Hospital * Area of Residence

			Area of Residence			Total
			Urban	Semi Urban	Rural	
Government Hospitals	Medical College	Count	48	24	48	120
		% within Nature and Type of Hospital	40.0%	20.0%	40.0%	100.0%
	District Hospital	Count	24	48	0	72
		% within Nature and Type of Hospital	33.3%	66.7%	0.0%	100.0%
	Taluk Hospital	Count	24	0	24	48
		% within Nature and Type of Hospital	50.0%	0.0%	50.0%	100.0%
	Primary Health Centre	Count	0	0	24	24
		% within Nature and Type of Hospital	0.0%	0.0%	100.0%	100.0%
	Others	Count	24	24	0	48
		% within Nature and Type of Hospital	50.0%	50.0%	0.0%	100.0%
Private Hospitals	Medical Colleges	Count	48	0	0	48
		% within Nature and Type of Hospital	100.0%	0.0%	0.0%	100.0%
	Multi Speciality	Count	24	48	23	95
		% within Nature and Type of Hospital	25.3%	50.5%	24.2%	100.0%
	Super Speciality	Count	23	24	48	95
		% within Nature and Type of Hospital	24.2%	25.3%	50.5%	100.0%
Total		Count	215	168	167	550
		% within Nature and Type of Hospital	39.1%	30.5%	30.4%	100.0%

Source: Survey Data

The following Table represents area of hospitals where they are located.

Table 4.9 Nature and Type of Hospital * Area of Hospitals

			Area of Hospitals			Total
			Urban	Semi Urban	Rural	
Government Hospitals	Medical College	Count	120	0	0	120
		% within Nature and Type of Hospital	100.0%	0.0%	0.0%	100.0%
	District Hospital	Count	49	23	0	72
		% within Nature and Type of Hospital	68.1%	31.9%	0.0%	100.0%
	Taluk Hospital	Count	0	24	24	48
		% within Nature and Type of Hospital	0.0%	50.0%	50.0%	100.0%
	Primary Health Centre	Count	0	0	24	24
		% within Nature and Type of Hospital	0.0%	0.0%	100.0%	100.0%
	Others	Count	48	0	0	48
		% within Nature and Type of Hospital	100.0%	0.0%	0.0%	100.0%
Private Hospitals	Medical Colleges	Count	48	0	0	48
		% within Nature and Type of Hospital	100.0%	0.0%	0.0%	100.0%
	Multi speciality	Count	95	0	0	95
		% within Nature and Type of Hospital	100.0%	0.0%	0.0%	100.0%
	Super Speciality	Count	23	0	72	95
		% within Nature and Type of Hospital	24.2%	0.0%	75.8%	100.0%
Total		Count	383	47	120	550
		% within Nature and Type of Hospital	69.6%	8.5%	21.8%	100.0%

Source: Survey Data

Out of the Patients selected 69.60 per cent preferred hospitals in the Urban area and 8.5 per cent preferred Semi urban and 21.8 per cent preferred hospitals in the rural area.

4.9 Area of Hospital

4.10 Category of Treatment

Table 4.10 describes that, out of the selected patients large number of patients (47.80 per cent) visited hospitals is for surgical needs, 30.40 per cent for other medical needs, 21.8 per cent visits for maternity purposes and those who selected Government medical college 60 per cent of were in the category of surgical needs.

4.11 Frequency of Visit

Table 4.11 depicts the frequency of visit by the respondents. Regarding the frequency of visit 39.30 per cent visited hospitals twice in a month and26.4 per cent visited hospital when there is a need and 25.8 per cent visited once in a week and 8.5 per cent visited once in a month.

4.12 Source of Information

From the table we can see that, out of the patients selected, 39.1 per cent of the patients came to know about hospitals from their friends, whereas 26.40 per cent get information from medical professionals and 17.1 per cent came to know about hospitals from their relatives and 8.7 per cent got information from Ex – patients.

4.13 Factors Influencing Selection of Hospitals

Before selecting a hospital people will analyse different factors. These factors will act as a determining force in the selection of hospitals. Here we will discuss

The following table represents the category in which patients had undertaken treatment.

Table 4.10 Nature and Type of Hospital * Category of Treatment

			Category of Treatment			Total
			Surgical	Medical	Maternity	
Government Hospitals	Medical College	Count	72	24	24	120
		% within Nature and Type of Hospital	60.0%	20.0%	20.0%	100.0%
	District Hospital	Count	25	23	24	72
		% within Nature and Type of Hospital	34.7%	31.9%	33.3%	100.0%
	Taluk Hospital	Count	24	24	0	48
		% within Nature and Type of Hospital	50.0%	50.0%	0.0%	100.0%
	Primary Health Centre	Count	0	0	24	24
		% within Nature and Type of Hospital	0.0%	0.0%	100.0%	100.0%
	Others	Count	24	0	24	48
		% within Nature and Type of Hospital	50.0%	0.0%	50.0%	100.0%
Private Hospitals	Medical Colleges	Count	24	24	0	48
		% within Nature and Type of Hospital	50.0%	50.0%	0.0%	100.0%
	Multi Speciality	Count	47	48	0	95
		% within Nature and Type of Hospital	49.5%	50.5%	0.0%	100.0%
	Super Speciality	Count	47	24	24	95
		% within Nature and Type of Hospital	49.5%	25.3%	25.3%	100.0%
Total		Count	263	167	120	550
		% within Nature and Type of Hospital	47.8%	30.4%	21.8%	100.0%

Source: Survey Data

Table 4.11shows how frequently the respondents visits the hospitals

Table 4.11 Nature and Type of Hospital * Frequency of Health Checkup

			Frequency of Health Checkup				Total
			When there is a need	Once in a week	Twice in a Month	Once in a month	
Government Hospitals	Medical College	Count	48	24	24	24	120
		% within Nature and Type of Hospital	40.0%	20.0%	20.0%	20.0%	100.0%
	District Hospital	Count	25	23	24	0	72
		% within Nature and Type of Hospital	34.7%	31.9%	33.3%	0.0%	100.0%
	Taluk Hospital	Count	24	24	0	0	48
		% within Nature and Type of Hospital	50.0%	50.0%	0.0%	0.0%	100.0%
	Primary Health Centre	Count	24	0	0	0	24
		% within Nature and Type of Hospital	100.0%	0.0%	0.0%	0.0%	100.0%
	Others	Count	24	24	0	0	48
		% within Nature and Type of Hospital	50.0%	50.0%	0.0%	0.0%	100.0%
Private Hospitals	Medical Colleges	Count	0	24	24	0	48
		% within Nature and Type of Hospital	0.0%	50.0%	50.0%	0.0%	100.0%
	Multi Speciality	Count	0	23	72	0	95
		% within Nature and Type of Hospital	0.0%	24.2%	75.8%	0.0%	100.0%
	Super Speciality	Count	0	0	72	23	95
		% within Nature and Type of Hospital	0.0%	0.0%	75.8%	24.2%	100.0%
Total		Count	145	142	216	47	550
		% within Nature and Type of Hospital	26.4%	25.8%	39.3%	8.5%	100.0%

Source: Survey Data

The following Tables shows how the respondents become aware of the hospitals

Table 4.12 Nature and Type of Hospital * Source of Information

			Source of Information					
			Proximity to Residence	Medical Professionals	Friends	Relatives	Ex-Patients	Total
Government Hospitals	Medical College	Count	48	24	24	0	24	120
		% within Nature and Type of Hospital	40.0%	20.0%	20.0%	0.0%	20.0%	100.0%
	District Hospital	Count	0	25	24	23	0	72
		% within Nature and Type of Hospital	0.0%	34.7%	33.3%	31.9%	0.0%	100.0%
	Taluk Hospital	Count	0	48	0	0	0	48
		% within Nature and Type of Hospital	0.0%	100.0%	0.0%	0.0%	0.0%	100.0%
	Primary Health Centre	Count	0	0	24	0	0	24
		% within Nature and Type of Hospital	0.0%	0.0%	100.0%	0.0%	0.0%	100.0%
	Others	Count	0	24	24	0	0	48
		% within Nature and Type of Hospital	0.0%	50.0%	50.0%	0.0%	0.0%	100.0%
Private Hospitals	Medical Colleges	Count	0	24	0	24	0	48
		% within Nature and Type of Hospital	0.0%	50.0%	0.0%	50.0%	0.0%	100.0%
	Multi speciality	Count	0	0	47	24	24	95
		% within Nature and Type of Hospital	0.0%	0.0%	49.5%	25.3%	25.3%	100.0%
	Super Speciality	Count	0	0	72	23	0	95
		% within Nature and Type of Hospital	0.0%	0.0%	75.8%	24.2%	0.0%	100.0%
Total		Count	48	145	215	94	48	550
		% within Nature and Type of Hospital	8.7%	26.4%	39.1%	17.1%	8.7%	100.0%

Source: Survey Data

about various factors that will affect the selection of hospitals by patients.

1. **Easy access:-** Most people prefer hospitals that are easily accessible to them. Easy access generally refers to proximity to residence and they can access it without much travelling.
2. **Image and Reputation of the hospital**: Hospital's policies, facilities, pricing structure etc. are determining factors contributing to thereputation of hospitals. Reputation is based on patient's perceptions of an organization. Reputation is the sum of a set of attributes assigned to an organization These attributes include the quality of the product or service, confidence, ethical conduct, management and leadership, social responsibility and biomedical innovation and research.
3. **Augmented facilities and care available in the hospital:** 'Augmented' means enhanced version of anything. People will prefer hospitals which provide augmented facilities and care to their patients
4. **Doctors' Qualification (Specialisation):** The doctors should be competent enough so as to satisfy the patients. Competency includes Medical Knowledge, Practice-based Learning and Improvement, Interpersonal and Communication Skills, Professionalism and System-based Practices. The competency level of doctors is an important factor that affects the satisfaction level
5. **Quality of treatment:** People usually have a preference to quality goods. It is also thesame

in the case of services. People always prefer hospitals that provide quality treatment.

6. **Reasonable and Lower charges compared to other hospitals**: If Quality treatment is available at a lesser price, people will opt for it. So hospitals should take utmost care in determining the charges for their services. Hospitals that provide quality services at a reasonable rate will have an upper hand in the society.

7. **Availability of Health insurance schemes:** Nowadays most people have health insurance schemes. So people having insurance policy will opt hospitals that are listed by the insurance companies.

8. **Emergency situations.** In the case of Emergency, they wouldn't go for preferences; there, they only consider accessibility, provided the hospitals has facility to handle emergencies.

9. **Reference/advice by Private Physicians or Family Doctor:-** Another influencing factor is advice from their family doctors.

10. **Advice of Ex- Patients, family members, friends and relatives**: it is a general practice that people will take advice from those who have availed the services. Most people select hospitals based on the opinion given by ex-patients, family members etc.

Here, the respondents were asked to rank these factors according to their preference. To assess the statistical significance of the factors influencing the selection of the Hospitals, Friedman test has been done to test the following hypotheses

H0: There is no significant difference in the factors affecting the selection ofhospital by the patients of hospitals in Kerala

H1: There is significant difference in the factors affecting the selection ofhospital by the patients of hospitals in Kerala.

Table 4.13 Mean Ranks for Factors influencing selection of Hospitals

	Mean Rank
Easy access	4.55
Image and Reputation of the hospital.	4.12
Augmented facilities and care available in the hospital.	**3.77**
Doctors Qualification (Specialisation)	**3.87**
Quality of treatment	4.23
Reasonable and Lower charges compared to other hospitals.	5.27
Availability of Health insurance schemes	6.26
Emergency situations.	6.88
Reference/advice by Private Physicians or Family Doctor	7.14
Advice of Ex- Patients, family members, friends andrelatives who have taken treatment earlier.	**8.92**

Source: Survey Data

From Table 4.13 it is clear that Augmented Facilities and care in the hospital have a mean rank of 3.77, which is the lowest one. Lowest mean, rank means it has the highest preference. So Augmented facilities and care in the hospital is the most dominant factor that influences the preference of the patient to select a hospital. Doctors' Qualification is the second dominant factor. Advice of Ex-Patients, Family members, Friends and Relatives who have taken treatment earlier has the least preference as it has the highest mean score.

Table 4.14 Friedman Test for the Preference of Factors Influencing Selection of Hospitals

Test Statistics[a]	
N	550
Chi-Square	1619.757
df	9
Asymp. Sig.	**.000**

Source: Survey Data

*Significant at 5 per cent level

The Friedman chi-square provides a value of 1619.757 which is statistically significant at 5 per cent level of significance ($p=0.000<0.05$). It means that there is significant difference among the mean ranks of the responses of selected patients and their preferences towards the selection of a hospital

4.14 Augmented Facilities and Care Available among Government and Private Sector Hospitals

Augmented facilities and care available at Government and Private sector hospitalsact as determinant forces in the selection of hospitals. The augmented facilities available may differ among various types of hospitals.

The Mann Whitney U Test, sometimes called the *MannWhitney* Wilcoxon *Test* or the Wilcoxon Rank Sum *Test,* is used to *test* whether two samples are likely to derive from the same population (i.e., that the two populations have the same shape). The Mann-Whitney U Test is used to compare differences between two independent groups when the dependent variable is either ordinal or continuous, but not normally distributed.

Table 4.15 Augmented Facilities Available in Government and Private Sector Hospitals

Ranks				
	Govt./Pvt.	*N*	*Mean Rank*	*Sum of Ranks*
Augmented facilities and care available in the hospital.	Government/Public Sector	264	280.10	73946.00
	Private Sector	286	271.26	77579.00
	Total	550		

Table 4.16 Mann Whitney test

Test Statistics[a]	
	Augmented facilities and care available in the hospital.
Mann-Whitney U	36538.000
Wilcoxon W	77579.000
Z	-.694
Asymp. Sig. (2-tailed)	.487

Source: Survey Data

As per the table for augmented facilities and care available in the hospital among all hospitals the lowest mean rank goes to private sector hospitals, which shows that when compared to government hospitals, private sector hospitals provide better augmented facilities and care available in the hospitals. But the mean rank variation is not found significant as P>.05 in the Mann Whitney U test.

This factor is again considered among various government and private sector hospitals with Kruskal Wallis test as the category (type of hospital) is having more than two groups.

The hypothesis can be stated as

H0 : There is no significant difference in the augmented facilities and care available for thepatients of different hospitals.

H1 : There is significant difference in the augmented facilities and care available for thepatients of different hospitals.

Table 4.17 Augmented Facilities Available in Government and Private Sector Hospitals

Ranks			
	Nature and Type of Hospital	*N*	*Mean Rank*
Augmented facilities and care available in the hospital.	Medical College	120	266.60
	District Hospital	72	278.03
	Taluk Hospital	48	330.50
	Primary Health Centre	24	253.00
	Others	48	253.00
	Private Medical Colleges	48	360.25
	Pvt.Multi-Speciality hospitals	95	299.24
	Private Super speciality	95	**207.53**
	Total	550	

Source: Survey Data

Table 4.18 Kruskal Wallis Test

	q14.3
Chi-Square	46.212
df	7
Asymp. Sig.	.000

a. Kruskal Wallis Test

b. Grouping Variable: Nature and Type of Hospital

*Source: Survey Data*Significant at 5 per cent level*

Regarding the augmented facilities among all hospitals the lowest mean rank goes to private super speciality hospitals, which shows, when compared to other hospitals private super speciality hospitals provide better augmented facilities than others. Further, the mean rank variation is found significant, as $P < .05$ in the Kruskal Wallis test.

4.15 Multiple Discriminant Analysis

A Discriminant Function is a linear combination of the predictorvariables that provide the best discrimination between the groups. Thevariables with high coefficients, and pooled within-group correlation betweendiscriminating variables and Discriminant function, will be used to identify theimportant variables.

As the first part in Discriminant Analysis, the Tests of Equality of GroupMeans is done to validate the power of each variable to the Discriminantfunction. The following table presents the results of tests of equality of groupmeans.

4.15.1 Discriminant Analysis for Finding out the Most Critical Factor that Create Satisfaction among Customers of Government Sector and Private Sector Hospitals

Discriminant analysis is used here to find out the most critical factor that creates satisfaction among patients.

1) **Level of Satisfaction on Nursing care:** Patient centred nursing care should be given to every patient. Care plans should be made to ensure that patients receive evidence-based holistic care. Nursing diagnosesshould be standardized to ensure quality care. Nursing interventions should be tailored to meet the physical, psychological, and social needs of the individual patient.

2) **Level of Satisfaction on Doctor's competence and medical care:** The doctors should be competent enough so as to satisfy the patients. Competency includesMedical Knowledge, Practice-based Learning and Improvement, Interpersonal and Communication Skills, Professionalism and system-based Practices. Competency level of doctors is an important factor that affects the satisfaction level.

3) **Level of Satisfaction on Supportive services:** Supportive services in a hospital include Nutrition and Dietary services, Pharmacy, Medical records, Laundry services and Housekeeping, Transportation, Mortuary, Communication system, Energy conservation methods, and Cost containment measures. These

supportive services should be properly managed so as to enhance the level of satisfaction

4) **Level of Satisfaction on Discharge process and billing System:** The discharge process is a key activity in In-Patient management at any hospital. Automaton of billing helps in making the discharge process more easy and comfortable.

5) **Level of Satisfaction on Hospital charges**: Hospital charges include the cost of lab tests, X-rays, surgical procedures, operating room and post-surgical costs, medications, and doctors' and specialists' fees. The various costs should be fair and reasonable so as to attract customers or patients

6) **Level of Satisfaction with equipment and instruments**: Availability of most modern equipments is a requisite for delivering proper treatments. Some of the equipment itemsrequired are medical imaging equipment, such as Radiography (X-ray machine), Computed Tomography (CT scan), Magnetic Resonance Imaging (MRI scan), ultrasound, and Echocardiography. Patients will be more satisfied if there the most modern techniques are available for treatment.

7) **Intensive Care Unit facility**: ICU is another factor that will influence the patient satisfaction level.Intensive Care Unit (ICU) is a specialised facility dedicated to patients who require intensive monitoring, nursing care and complex respiratory support. The ICU is staffed 24 hours a day by board-certified specialists and seasoned

critical care nurses, nurse practitioners and physician assistants, who are committed to providing quality clinical care.

8) **Pharmacy facility**: Pharmacy is the department of the hospital which deals with the procurement, storage, compounding, dispensing, manufacturing, testing, packaging, and distribution of drugs. The practice of pharmacy within the hospitals under the supervision of a professional pharmacist, is known as hospital pharmacy. People will prefer hospitals with proper pharmacy facilities.

9) **Knowledge of the staff:** The real asset of any institution is its human resources. Skill and knowledge of the employee is an important factor in determining the satisfaction level of its employees. So, every institution should take appropriate measures to enhance the knowledge and skill of its employees.

10) **Cleanliness and hygiene:** Cleanliness and hygiene is important in any public place, but, in hospitals and medical practices, it is critical due to the fact that the spread of germs can endanger individuals who are already at risk. People will prefer hospitals with cleanliness and hygiene. So, the satisfaction level is directly related with cleanliness and hygiene.

11) **Confidence and support given**: At the stage of illness people feel disturbed and desperate. Confidence and support given by the medical teamis a must for the speedy recovery of the patients. So it also acts as a yardstick for satisfaction level.

12) **Follow up**: Proper follow-up is required to maintain its customers. Proper follow-up will create a feel that they are considered and it will enhance the satisfaction level.

13) **Parking facility**: Nowadays,people will consider hospitals with parking facilities. It act as a main determinant in selecting the hospital

The following Hypothesis is tested with the help of Discriminant analysis:

H0: There is no significant difference in the factor responsible for the satisfaction of patients of Private and Government Hospitals.

H1: There is significant difference in the factor responsible for the satisfaction of patients of Private and Government Hospitals.

Table 4.19: Wilks' Lambda

Test of Function(s)	*Wilks' Lambda*	*Chi-square*	*df*	*Sig.*
1	.109	1202.345	13	.000

Source: Survey Data

*Significant at 5 per cent level

Table 4.20: Standardized Canonical Discriminant Function Coefficients

	Function
	1
Level of Satisfaction on Nursing care	.349
Level of Satisfaction on Doctors' competence and medical care	.495
Level of Satisfaction on Supportive services	.368
Level of Satisfaction on Discharge process and billing System	.111
Level of Satisfaction on Hospital charges (Cost)	.677
Level of Satisfaction on Equipment and instruments	-.298
Intensive Care Unit facility	-1.866
Pharmacy facility	-.172
Knowledge of the staff	1.890
Cleanliness and hygiene	.697
Confidenceand support given to me	.561
Follow-up	**-2.429**
Parking facility	.630

Source: Survey Data

Table 4.21: Functions at Group Centroids

Nature and Type of Hospitals	*Function*
	1
Government Hospitals	-2.977
Private Hospitals	2.748

Unstandardized canonical discriminant functions evaluated at group means

Source: Survey Data

The factors affecting the satisfaction among patients of public and private sector hospitals were explained by applying multiple discriminant analysis. From the statistics of discriminant analysis, the Wilks Lambda characterised by the chi-square was found significant (Wilks Lambda .109 with Chi –square 1202.345, $P<0.05$).

So, the model was found valid for interpretation. The output also gave a centroid matrix, where the negative co-efficient belonged to Government sector hospitals and the positive co-efficient to private sector hospitals. From the standardised canonical discriminant functions, it was seen that the highest negative co-efficient was -2.429, the follow up processand the second highest negative co-efficient was -1.866, Intensive Care Unit facility. But the highest positive co-efficient was 1.890 for knowledge of the staff and the second highest positive co-efficient 0.697 for Cleanliness and hygiene. Therefore, it could be concluded that in Government sector hospitals Follow-up process and Intensive care unit facility and in private sector hospitals knowledge of the staff, Cleanliness and hygiene, were the critical factors; and these factors created more satisfaction among patients in these two hospital sectors

4.16 Loyalty of Patients among Government and Private Hospitals

Here loyalty means the quality of being faithful to someone or something else. Loyal customers will stick to a particular product or service. They will not switch products in normal case. This is also the case of hospitals. Generally identified loyalties in the case of the service sector are CognitiveLoyalty, Affective Loyalty, Intention Loyalty and Behavioural Loyalty

4.16.1 Cognitive Loyalty

Cognitive Loyalty is the first loyalty phase. Loyalty in this stage, derives from previous/explicit knowledge or recent information based on experiences. Cognitive Loyalty is mainly based on the offerings in relation to price. Once the cost-to-benefit ratio is worse than what your competitors offer, the client will switch to a better price. In this study Cognitive loyalty is measured with the help of four statements

1) Will consider the hospital as my first choice in my next visit;
2) Will consider the hospital as my primary choice in my next visit;
3) Service of this hospital is better thanthat of others;
4) Willingness to pay more to this hospital next time;

4.16.2 *Affective Loyalty*

This stage of consumer loyalty is characterized by strong brand awareness. Affective loyalty is achieved through matching the brand attributes and services to consumer expectations. The following statements are used to measure the affective loyalty

1) Likes to visit the Hospital;
2) Believes most in this hospital;
3) Prefers the hospital more than others;
4) Appreciates this hospital in this city.

4.16.3 Intention Loyalty

Intention Loyalty of the patients is measured with the help of following statements.

1) Intends to visit this hospital again;
2) Intends to recommend this hospital to others;

3) Intends to say good thing about this hospital to others;
4) Intends to give feedback about this hospital.

4.16.4 Behavioural Loyalty

Behavioural loyalty is said to present when a customer continues to buy or use a particular product, service or brand . For analysing this type of loyalty, the following statements are provided in the Interview Schedule

1) Come to this hospital when I become sick,
2) Likes to spend more to stay in this hospital;
3) More visits at this hospital compared to others;
4) Use more of the Services in this hospital compared to others;

4.17 Multivariate Analysis of Variance

To evaluate the variations in the Loyalty level of patients, leading to satisfaction, a Multivariate Analysis of Variance (MANOVA) was applied.The importance of MANOVA is seen widely in decisions related to a set of related variables observed in more than two groups. If ANOVA is used it may give the result that a variable is not significant, but MANOVA may provide reasons to say that the variable is significant in the presence of all variables taken together. Also, by doing MANOVA, the real understanding of the possible variations is made more pronounced.

It was aimed to analyse the response on such problems for explaining the possible deviations observed among patients of different hospitals. The MANOVA for this group of four factors, by types of hospitals and loyalty types was considered. To explain the possible variations observed in these variables, across different hospitals under survey, MANOVA for this bundle of four variables by onefactor (type of hospitals) was considered. This procedure was to test the null hypothesis about the effect of factor variables on the means of the bundle of variables.

The test of MANOVA was used here to test the following hypotheses.

H0: There is no variation in the mean scores obtained for the set of variablesdescribing the loyalty across various types of hospitals.

H1: There is significant variation in the mean scores obtained for the set ofvariables describing the loyalty across various types of hospitals.

The output derived from MANOVA is depicted in the following Table

Table 4.22: Multivariate Tests[a]

Effect		*Value*	*F*	*Hypothesis df*	*Error df*	*Sig.*
Nature and	Pillai's Trace	1.396	41.528	28.000	2168.000	.000
Type of	Wilks' Lambda	.070	75.810	28.000	1944.814	.000
Hospital	Hotelling's Trace	7.244	139.067	28.000	2150.000	.000
	Roy's Largest Root	6.406	496.030[c]	7.000	542.000	.000

a. Design: Intercept + Nature and Type of Hospital

b. Exact statistic

c. The statistic is an upper bound on F that yields a lower bound on the significance level.

Source: Survey Data

*Significant at 5 per cent level

Table 4.23 Tests of Between-Subjects Effects

Source	*Dependent Variable*	*Type I Sum of Squares*	*df*	*Mean Square*	*F*	*Sig.*
Nature and Type of Hospital	Cognitive Loyalty	22345.410	7	3192.201	229.597	.000
	Affective Loyalty	25580.174	7	3654.311	442.820	.000
	Intention Loyalty	18118.015	7	2588.288	258.094	.000
	Behavioural Loyalty	17641.558	7	2520.223	220.734	.000
Error	Cognitive Loyalty	7535.688	542	13.903		
	Affective Loyalty	4472.780	542	8.252		
	Intention Loyalty	5435.439	542	10.028		
	Behavioural Loyalty	6188.262	542	11.417		
Total	Cognitive Loyalty	214840.000	550			
	Affective Loyalty	216077.000	550			
	Intention Loyalty	184208.000	550			
	Behavioural Loyalty	177955.000	550			
Total	Cognitive Loyalty	29881.098	549			
	Affective Loyalty	30052.955	549			
	Intention Loyalty	23553.455	549			
	Behavioural Loyalty	23829.820	549			

a. R Squared = .748 (Adjusted R Squared = .745)

b. R Squared = .851 (Adjusted R Squared = .849)

c. R Squared = .769 (Adjusted R Squared = .766)

d. R Squared = .740 (Adjusted R Squared = .737)

Source: Survey Data

*Significant at 5 per cent level

The summary statistics of mean scores found in the different types of hospitals is presented in the following table:

Table 4.24 Estimated Marginal Means- Hospital-Wise

Dependent Variable	*Nature and Type of Hospital*	*Mean*	*Std. Error*	*95% Confidence Interval*	
				Lower Bound	*Upper Bound*
Cognitive	Medical College	11.000	.340	10.331	11.669
Loyalty	District Hospital	14.097	.439	13.234	14.960
	Taluk Hospital	12.000	.538	10.943	13.057
	Primary Health Centre	10.000	.761	8.505	11.495
	Others	24.500	.538	23.443	25.557
	Private Medical colleges	25.000	.538	23.943	26.057
	Private Multi-Speciality hospitals	**26.242**	.383	25.491	26.994
	Private Super Speciality	21.747	.383	20.996	22.499
Affective	Medical College	11.600	.262	11.085	12.115
Loyalty	District Hospital	13.542	.339	12.877	14.207
	Taluk Hospital	10.500	.415	9.686	11.314
	Primary Health centre	8.000	.586	6.848	9.152
	Others	25.000	.415	24.186	25.814
	Private Medical Colleges	26.500	.415	25.686	27.314
	Private. Multi-Speciality Hospitals	**26.737**	.295	26.158	27.316
	Private Super Speciality	21.474	.295	20.895	22.053
Intention	Medical College	12.800	.289	12.232	13.368
Loyalty	District Hospital	13.528	.373	12.795	14.261
	Taluk Hospital	8.500	.457	7.602	9.398
	Primary Health centre	5.000	.646	3.730	6.270
	Others	22.000	.457	21.102	22.898
	Private Medical colleges	**24.500**	.457	23.602	25.398
	Private Multi-Speciality hospitals	22.253	.325	21.614	22.891
	Private Super Speciality	21.221	.325	20.583	21.859
Behavioural	Medical College	11.200	.308	10.594	11.806
Loyalty	District Hospital	12.556	.398	11.773	13.338

Taluk Hospital	10.000	.488	9.042	10.958
Primary Health centre	8.000	.690	6.645	9.355
Others	23.500	.488	22.542	24.458
Private Medical colleges	21.000	.488	20.042	21.958
Private Multi-Speciality hospitals	**23.716**	.347	23.035	24.397
Private Super Speciality	19.979	.347	19.298	20.660

Source: Survey Data

The Variation in all the loyalty factors among different type of hospitals were tested by using MANOVA. Based on the highest mean score it was observed that Private Multi-Speciality had higher Cognitive, Affective and behavioural loyalty than that of others, whereas Private medical college has a higher Intention Loyalty.

It is a generally the accepted procedure to take Wilks' Lambda for testinghypothesis from among the four standard statistics reported above. However, from some recent studies, it is seen that Pillai's Trace is more powerful than the other tests.From the output, it is clear that all the four test statistics (Pillai's Trace, Wilks' Lambda, Hotelling's Trace, Roy's Largest Root) used for multivariate analysis provide significant F values at 5 per cent level ($p<0.05$). Hence, the null hypothesis is rejected. It can thus be concluded that there exists significant difference in the mean scores obtained for the set of variables determining patient loyalty among the different types of hospitals under study.

4.18 Factors Influencing Patient Trust in Hospitals

Patients trust in the hospital means how they trust the services of hospitals. Patient Trust level can be considered as a barometer that measures the confidence level and loyalty level. To measure the trust level various statements such as, this hospital is honest, I believe the custom of this hospital, I am ready to rank this hospital as good one, I assure this hospital provides the best service to all, the information provided by the hospital is correct, I strongly believes that, this hospital is working as a service motive not as a business motive, I trust the doctors and nurses, these hospitals do the treatment as their service motive, there is no hidden charges in the billing. The doctors and nurses are always try their level best to save the patient's life

The variation of Patients Trust by their area of residence is tested with ANOVA and the output is presented in Table 4.25.

Table 4.25: Tests of Between-Subjects Effects

Dependent Variable: Patients' Trust					
Source	*Type I Sum of Squares*	*df*	*Mean Square*	*F*	*Sig.*
Area of Residence	7884.448	2	3942.224	14.305	.000
Error	150739.916	547	275.576		

a. R Squared = .050 (Adjusted R Squared = .046)

Source: Survey Data

*Significant at 5 per cent level

Table 4.26 : Estimated Marginal Means-Area of Residence Wise Patient's Trust

Dependent Variable: Patients' Trust				
Area of Residence	*Mean*	*Std. Error*	*95% Confidence Interval*	
			Lower Bound	*Upper Bound*
Urban	47.735	1.132	45.511	49.959
Semi Urban	**49.274**	1.281	46.758	51.790
Rural	40.293	1.285	37.770	42.817

Source: Survey Data

Regarding the Patient Trust towards hospitals , it is found to have more influence among Semi Urban Patients (Mean Score 49.274). The mean score variation is found significant at 5 per cent level($P<0.05$).

4.19 Factors influencing the Overall Satisfaction of Patients-CoreVariables

To measure the overall satisfaction level, core Service Quality variables such as Tangibility, Reliability, Responsiveness, Assurance, Empathy, Courtesy and Communication were identified and various statement based on this is given to respondents. Various statements are given to the respondents.

Step-wise Multiple Regression is used to test the statistical validity of the following Hypotheses

H0: There is no significant dependence between the overall satisfaction of patients and the Core service factors such as Empathy, Responsiveness, Communication, Reliability, Access and Tangibility

H1: There issignificant dependence between the overall satisfaction of patients and the Core service factors empathy responsiveness communication Reliability, Access and Tangibility.

Table 4.27: Model Summary–Overall Satisfaction

Model	*R*	*R Square*	*Adjusted R Square*	*Std. Error of the Estimate*
6	.980[f]	.961	.960	4.37188

Source: Survey Data

Table 4.28: ANOVA - Overall Satisfaction

	Model	*Sum of Squares*	*df*	*Mean Square*	*F*	*Sig.*
6	Regression	252581.492	6	42096.915	2202.487	.000[g]
	Residual	10378.552	543	19.113		
	Total	262960.044	549			

Source: Survey Data

*Significant at 5 per cent level

Table 4.29: Coefficients- Overall Satisfaction

Model		*Unstandardized Coefficients*		*Standardized Coefficients*	*t*	*Sig.*
		B	*Std. Error*	*Beta*		
6	(Constant)	-8.501	.960		-8.853	.000
	Empathy	1.379	.054	.581	25.596	.000
	Responsiveness	.568	.071	.248	7.988	.000
	Communication	.230	.092	.057	2.495	.013
	Reliability	.347	.047	.200	7.320	.000
	Access	-.514	.081	-.193	-6.333	.000
	Tangibility	.269	.077	.128	3.489	.001

a. Dependent Variable: Overall Satisfaction

Source: Survey Data

*Significant at 5 per cent level

The influence of independent variables related to overall satisfaction of patients is examined withthe help of Stepwise Multiple Regression Model. The model summary table shows that the value of R^2 is 0.961, which means 96 per cent of the influence on overall satisfaction is due to the factors such as Empathy, Responsiveness, Communication, Reliability, Access and Tangibility. The value of F statistics in ANOVA is **2202.487** which is found significant at 5 per cent level, indicates that the regression model is fitted reasonably.

Further, the Co-efficient Matrix of the sixth model of Regression indicates that Empathy, Responsiveness,

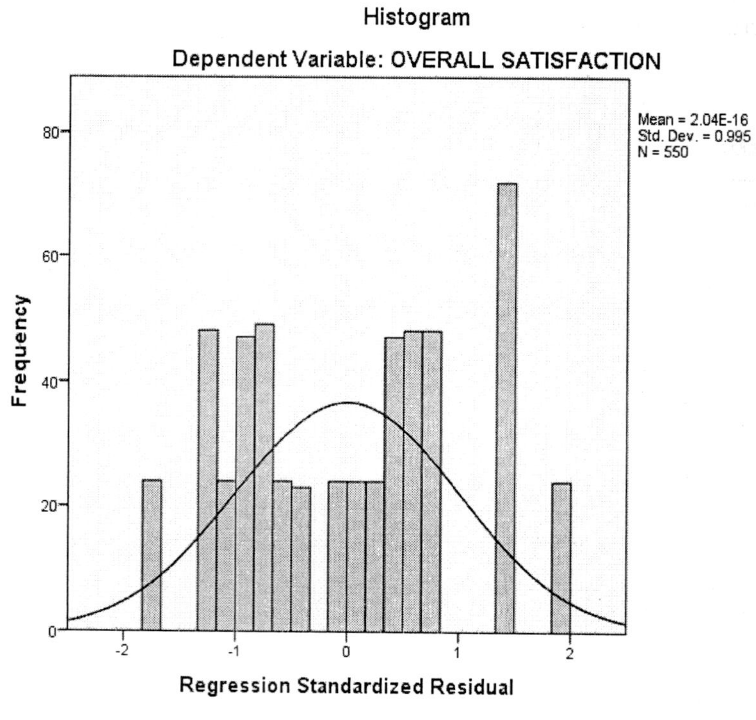

Figure 4.1

Communication, Reliability, Access and Tangibility influence the overall satisfaction of the patients, as the values of Beta co-efficient of these factors are found significant (t values with P<.05) in all these cases.

Therefore, the fitted Regression model is Overall satisfaction (y) = -8.501, + 1.379 Empathy, +.568 Responsiveness, +.230 Communication, +.347 Reliability, -.514 Access, +.269 Tangibility

4.20 Modern Service Quality Factors

Modern Service Quality factors include Personality factors, Managerial skill, Sustainable Services, Operation (Surgery Facility), Infrastructure and Information Technology. Various statements have been given to the respondents and their responses are analysed with the help of Stepwise Multiple Regression

Table 4.30: Model Summary- Overall satisfaction

Model	*R*	*R Square*	*Adjusted R Square*	*Std. Error of the Estimate*
5	.948[e]	.899	.898	6.98246

Source: Survey Data

Table 4.31: ANOVA-Overall Satisfaction

Model		*Sum of Squares*	*df*	*Mean Square*	*F*	*Sig.*
5	Regression	236437.463	5	47287.493	969.905	.000[f]
	Residual	26522.581	544	48.755		
	Total	262960.044	549			

a. Dependent Variable: Overall Satisfaction

Source: Survey Data

*Significant at 5 per cent level

Table 4.32: Coefficients of Overall Satisfaction

	Model	Unstandardized Coefficients		Standardized Coefficients			Collinearity Statistics	
		B	Std. Error	Beta	t	Sig.	Tolerance	VIF
	(Constant)	-16.199	1.176		-13.776	.000		
	Infrastructure Facility	1.255	.132	.407	9.539	.000	.102	9.833
	Personality Factor	1.572	.109	.458	14.391	.000	.183	5.459
5	Sustainable Services	1.118	.109	.334	10.222	.000	.173	5.768
	Information Technology	-.948	.145	-.278	-6.517	.000	.102	9.804
	Managerial Skill	.243	.106	.086	2.291	.022	.133	7.532

a. Dependent Variable: Overall Satisfaction

Source: Survey Data

*Significant at 5 per cent level

The influence of independent variables related to the overall Satisfaction of patients is examined withthe help of the stepwise Multiple Regression Model. The Model Summary table shows that the value of R^2 is .899, which meansthat 89.9 per cent of the influence on overall satisfaction is due to the factors such as Infrastructure facility, Personality Factor, Sustainable Factor, Information Technology and Managerial Skill. The value of F statistics in ANOVA is 969.905 which is found significant at 5 per cent level, indicates that the Regression Model is fitted reasonably.

Further, the Co-efficient Matrix of Regression indicates that Infrastructure Facility, Personality Factor, Sustainable Factor, Information Technology and

Managerial Skill influence the Overall satisfaction of the patients, as the beta coefficient of these factors are found significant (t values with P<.05) in all these cases.

Therefore the fitted Regression model is Overall Satisfaction (y) = -16.199, +1.255 Infrastructure facility, +1.572 Personality Factor, +1.118 Sustainable factor, -.948 Information Technology, +.243 Managerial skill.

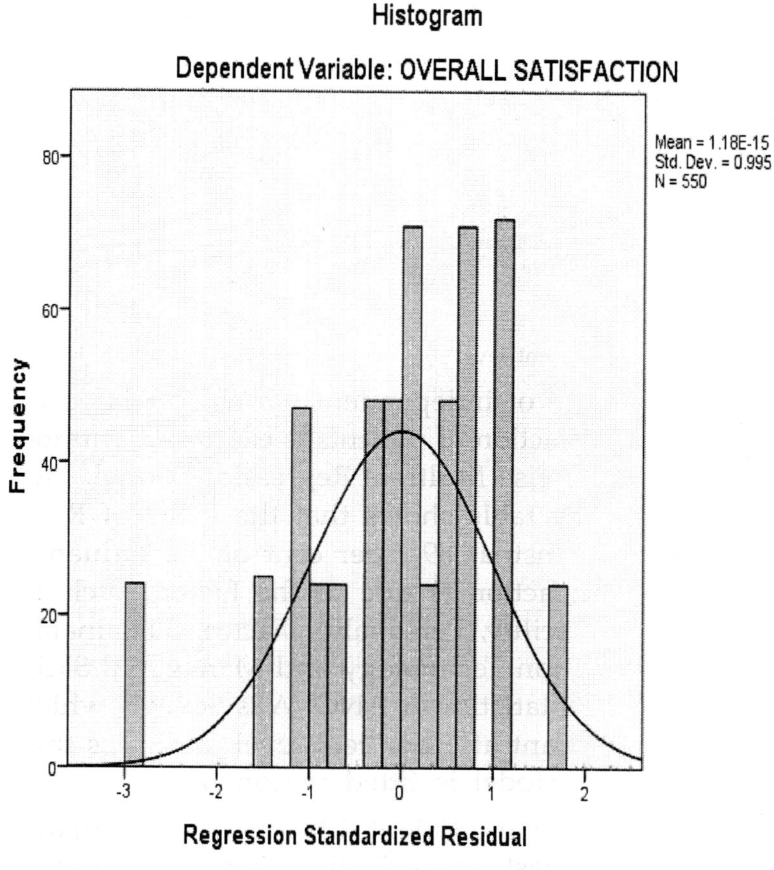

Figure 4.2

4.21 Problems Faced by the Patients causing Dissatisfaction

Discriminant analysis is used here to find out problems that may be faced by the patients, causingdissatisfaction among them

1. **Waiting time:** Waiting time refers to the time a patient waits in the hospital before being attended by themedical staff. Waiting time is an important indicator of quality of services offered by hospitals.Usually patients prefer hospitals with less waiting time especially in the case of non-emergency cases
2. **Cumbersome Procedural formalities for registration:** Patient registration is a complex process that requires a considerable amount of patient data input,including demographic information, personal and contact information, patient referral, appointment, scheduling and Collection of patient health history etc.
3. **Lack of infrastructural facilities:** Infrastructure facility refers to basic facilities available in the hospitals. Lack of infrastructure facility will cause dissatisfaction in the minds of patients.
4. **Lack of Cleanliness of the hospital:** Physical evidence is an important factor in Service Quality. Proper cleanliness and hygiene is a must for satisfaction. Lack of cleanliness will create dissatisfaction.
5. **Non Co-operation of attenders and sweepers:** To maintain a hygiene situation cooperation from the part of attenders and sweepers is

required. If they are not co–operative, it will ultimately lead to dissatisfaction.

6. **Inadequate space in patient rooms:** Another disappointing factor may be inadequate space in patient rooms. So management should take measures to provide spacious rooms.
7. **No Patient Relationship Management:** As after sales service has an important role in marketing Patient Relationship management is also a satisfaction factor. If there is no proper patient relationship management, it will lead to dissatisfaction.
8. **Lack of diagnostic amenities and equipment:** If there is no proper equipment it will lead to dissatisfaction among patients
9. **Lack of latest treatment methods:** In this modern era, people prefer treatments with the help of the most modern equipment. Lack of proper equipment will also lead to dissatisfaction
10. **Lack of expert (specialist) doctors;**In the era of specialisation people prefer specialists. Lack of specialist also causes disappointment for patients.
11. **Improper diagnosing of disease**:-Diagnose is the base of treatment. If diagnosis is not proper it will affect the entire treatment process and will lead to dissatisfaction
12. **Poor quality of treatment:** Satisfaction mainly lies on the quality of treatment. If proper treatment is not given, it will also cause dissatisfaction

13. **High cost of treatment/Exorbitant fees charged:** To satisfy patients treatment should be provided at reasonable rates. If exorbitant rates are charged, it will cause dissatisfaction.

14. **Advance payment:**If advance deposits are received it will also cause a feeling of insecurity and it will lead to dissatisfaction

15. **Mode of payments (Cash, Debit/Credit Card):** Modern payment options like payment through Debit / Credit card and UPI also should be made available.

Discriminant Analysis is used to test the following hypothesis

H0: There is no significant difference in the factors responsible for thedissatisfaction ofpatients of Private and Government Hospitals

H1: There is significant difference in the factors responsible for the dissatisfaction of patients of Private and Government Hospitals

Table 4.33: Wilks' Lambda – Dissatisfaction of Patients

Test of Function(s)	*Wilks' Lambda*	*Chi-square*	*df*	*Sig.*
1	.036	1797.272	15	.000

Table 4.34: Standardized Canonical Discriminant Function Coefficients- Dissatisfaction of Patients

	Function
	1
Waiting time	-3.472
Cumbersome Procedural formalities for registration	5.019
Lack of infrastructural facilities	-3.647
Lack of Cleanliness of the hospital	2.345
Non Co-operation of attenders and sweepers	-.985
Inadequate space in patient rooms	2.105
No Patient Relationship Management	-4.081
Lack of diagnostic amenities and equipment	**9.344**
Lack of latest treatment methods	-1.527
Lack of expert (specialist) doctors	**9.696**
Improper diagnosing of disease	**-11.634**
No proper and quality of treatment	**-4.304**
High cost of Treatment/Exorbitant fees charged	.376
Advance payment	1.500
Mode of payments (Cash, Debit/Credit Card)	2.068

Source: Survey Data

Table 4.35: Functions at Group Centroids

GOVT/PVT	Function
	1
Government	-5.379
Private	4.965

Unstandardized canonical discriminant functions evaluated at group means

Source: Survey Data

The various problems faced by patients of public and private sector hospitals were explained by applying multiple discriminant analysis. From the statistics of discriminant analysis, the Wilks Lambda characterised by the Chi-square was found significant (Wilks Lambda .036with chi –square 1797.272, P<0.05). So, the model was found valid for interpretation. The output also gave a centroid matrix, where the negative co-efficient belonged to Government sector hospitals and the positive co-efficient to private sector hospitals. From the standardised canonical discriminant function it was seen that the highest negative co-efficient was-**11.634,** for Improper diagnosing of disease, and the second highest negative co-efficient was **-4.304,** for poor quality of treatment. But the highest positive co-efficient was **9.696,**for Lack of expert (specialist) doctors and second highest positive co-efficient was **9.344** for Lack of diagnostic amenities and equipment. Therefore, it could be concluded that in Improper diagnosing of disease and No proper and poor quality of treatment in Government hospitals and Lack of expert (specialist) doctors and Lack of diagnostic amenities and equipment in private hospitals were the critical factors which created more dissatisfaction among patients.

4.22 Conclusion

In this chapter, factors affecting Service Quality of patients in Government and Private Sector hospitals has been analysed. Regarding the demographic profile, the majority of the patients are female and they have educational qualification upto SSLC and the majority of the patients are youngsters in the age group of 20-30. The majority of the patients are from urban area and majority among them have income between 2,00,001-5,00,000. The augmented facilities and care available in the hospitals are considered as the most dominant factor that influenced patients in the selection of hospitals. Among government and private hospitals, private super speciality hospitals provided better augmented care and facilities. In Government hospitals,Follow up process and Intensive care unit (ICU) facility were the critical factors that decided satisfaction, and knowledge of the staff and cleanliness and hygiene in the case of private sector hospitals. It is found that Private Multi-Speciality hospital have higher cognitive, affective and behavioural loyalty whereas private medical colleges has higher intention loyalty. The core variables affecting patients' satisfaction and their impact were identified by applying Stepwise Multiple Linear Regression. The influence of independent variables related to overall satisfaction of patients is examined with the help of Stepwise Multiple Regression model. It is found that among core service variables, Empathy, Responsiveness communication, Reliability, Access and Tangibility created more satisfaction among patients. Factors such as Personality, Managerial skill, Sustainable services, Operation (surgery) Facility, Infrastructure and Information technology were considered as Modern Service Quality factors.

Among facilities available (Modern Service Quality variables) in the hospitals, Personality, Managerial skill Sustainable Services, Operation (surgery) facility created more satisfaction. Various problems faced by patients of public and private sector hospitals were explained by applying multiple discriminant analysis. In Government hospitals Improper diagnosis and poor quality treatment caused dissatisfaction among patients, whereas in the case of private hospitals lack of specialist doctors and diagnostic amenities and equipment were the factors causing dissatisfaction.

REFERENCES

[1] Aaker, D. A. and Jacobson, R. (1994), "The financial information content of perceived service quality", Journal of Marketing Research, *e31*, May, 191-201.

[2] Archana Patel, Vijay Thawani & Kunda Gharpure, (2003). World Health Organisation, (Health Action International) In Medicine Pricing Affordability and Availability in Maharashtra.

[3] Ashok Vikhe-Patil, K.V. Somasundaram, and R.C. Goyal (2002). Current Health scenario in rural India,Aust. Journal of Rural Health, *10*, pp. 129–135.

[4] Berry, L. L., Parasuraman, A., and Zeithaml, V.A. (1988). The service quality puzzle,Business Horizons, pp. 36–44.

[5] Bhore Committee, (1946). "The Health Survey and development".

[6] Bolton, R.N., and James, H. D. (1991). "A longitudinal analysis of the impact of service changes on customer attitudes", Journal of Marketing, 55, pp. 1–9.

[7] Bopp, K. D. (1990). "How patients evaluate the quality of ambulatory medical encounters". Journal of Healthcare Marketing; 10:6–15.

[8] Conel, C., and Fletcther EAA, (1985). "An analysis of service quality at a student health centre". International Journal of Healthcare Quality Assurance 1985; 14, pp. 260–267.

[9] Donabedian, A., (1980). Explorations in Quality Assessment and Monitoring. Ann Arbor. MI: Health Administration Press.

[10] Fagare, G. J. (1991). Thesis titled "Impact and Assessment of National Health Policy with special reference to Chandgadtaluka."

[11] Gronroos, C., (1990). "A service quality model and its marketing implications". European Journal of Marketing 1990; 18: pp. 36–44.

[12] Parasuraman, A., Zeithaml, V.A., and Berry L.L., (1993). "A multiple items scale for measuring consumer perceptions of service quality". Journal of Retailing; *66*, pp.12–40.

[13] ShridharVamanSherigar (June-2005). "An Analytical study of the Quality of Patient services in some selected Hospitals in Mumbai."

[14] Tse, D. K., and Wilton, P. C. (1988) "Models of customer satisfaction formation".Journal of Marketing Research; 25, pp. 204–212.

[15] U.R. Mane-Patil (1995). Ph.D. thesis titled "Hospital Management" 51.

5

Summary of Findings, Conclusions and Suggestions

5.1 Introduction

'Quality' is usually considered as the outcome of satisfaction. In the study, an attempt is made to study the Service Quality of Hospitals in Kerala. Hospital business is growing day by day in Kerala,it is generally considered as a service oriented industry.

In modern days, most of the hospitals are turned into profit oriented ones. In this competitive world, competition among hospitals is also increasing. In the era of competition main concern is survival and success. When the urge for profit increases, quality of services is sacrificed and the patients have to suffer a lot.

Competition in the Hospital industry is growing at a vigorous rate in Kerala. As the competition increases the profitability of the hospitals is questioned. When profitability decreases some firms seek to introduce unethical practices in the medical field, some medical practitioners also supports these unethical practices. As the wealth of population increases the patients will become more quality conscious and they will demand better services. The main problem to be faced by the patient community in Kerala is the disparity in the quality of services offered by different types of hospitals. This study attempts to analyse the quality of services offered by different types of hospitals in Kerala. It also analyses the awareness level and satisfaction level of patients regarding the services offered by the hospitals in Kerala.

In this study, the population includes the patients of Government and Private sector hospitals in Kerala, out of this 550 patients were selected for the study.Two Stage Random sampling has been applied for the selection of sample patients. In the first stage one hospital has been selected from each type of hospital, and in the second stage the required number of patients have been selected proportionately from the list of patients visited in the month of January 2019.

Statistical methods such as Friedman Test, Kruskal Wallis Test, Mann Whitney U test, Multiple Discriminant Analysis, Multivariate Analysis of Variance (MANOVA), Stepwise Multiple Regression were used for establishing the relationship between the variables under study.

5.2 Findings

A. Demographic Profile of Patients

1. Out of the 550 selected patients, majority (56.4 per cent) were female and 43.6 per cent were male. 74.7 per cent of the patients in the private multi-speciality hospitals were male and 74.7

per cent patients in the private super speciality sector were female.

2. Regarding the age, themajority of the respondents (47.6 per cent) belonged to the age group of 20-40 and 4.4 per cent were above 80. Out of the patients who opted Government Medical College, 40 per cent belonged to the age group of 61-80. In the case of District hospitals 100 per cent were in the age group of 20-40. In the case of Taluk hospitals 50 per cent of respondents were in the age group of 20-40 and 50 per cent were in the age group of 41-60. In the case of Primary health centre 100 per cent have age above 80. In the case of Private medical college 50 per cent are below 20 and 50 per cent in the age group of 61-80.
3. Out of the 550 patients selected, 65.5 per cent were married ;and 21.5 were unmarried and 8.7 per cent were widower and 4.4 per cent were divorcee. Among those who opted Govt. medical colleges 80 per cent were married and 20 per cent were unmarried. Among the patients in Private Medical Colleges 50 per cent were unmarried and 50 per cent were divorcees. In the case of Primary Health Centre 100 per cent were married.
4. Regarding educational qualification, the majority of the respondents (34.7 per cent) had education up to SSLC 17.6 per cent were diploma holders, 30.2 per cent were graduates 8.7 per cent were post graduates, and 8.7 per cent held other educational qualification. Out of the patients who opted Government medical college 60 per

cent have educational qualification up to SSLC. In the case of District hospitals, 65.3 per cent were diploma holders. In the case of Taluk hospitals 50 per cent of respondents were Graduates, and 50 per cent held other degrees. In the case of Primary health centre, 100 per cent had educational qualification up to SSLC. In the case of Private medical college, 50 per cent had educational qualification upto SSLC and 50 per cent were Post Graduates.

5. From the study, it is clear that 26.2 per cent of the patients were self-employed and 22 per cent were Govt. employees and 21.6 per cent were Private employees and 13.1 per cent were professionals and 17.1 per cent were workers. Among the patients who opted Govt. medical colleges 60 per cent were self-employed and in the case of those who opted private medical colleges, 50 per cent were Government employees and 50 per cent were professionals.
6. Regarding income, out of the patients selected 39.1 per cent are in the group of Rs. 200001-500000; 34.9 per cent were in the income group Rs.100000-200000. Of those who selected Govt. medical college 40 per cent have income less than 100000 and 100 percent of those who selected primary health centres had income less than 100000.
7. A large numberof the respondants (39.10 per cent) were residing in urban area, 30.5 percent were from semi urban area and 30.4 per cent inrural area. Of those who selected private medical colleges, 100 per cent were from Urban areas.

8. Out of the patients selected 69.60 per cent preferred hospitals in the Urban area and 8.5 per cent preferred hospitals in Semi urban and 21.8 per cent preferred hospitals in the rural area.
9. Regarding the purpose of visit, a large number of patients (47.80 per cent) visited hospitals for Surgical needs, 30.40 per cent approached for other medical needs and21.8 per cent for maternity purposes and 60 per cent of those who selected Government medical college for surgical needs.
10. Regarding the frequency of visit; 39.30 per cent visited hospitals twice in a month, 26.4 per cent visited hospital when there is a need and 25.8 per cent visited hospitals once in a week and 8.5 per cent visited hospitals once in a month.
11. Out of the patients selected, 39.1 per cent of the patients came to know about hospitals from their friends, whereas 26.40 per cent got information from medical professionals and 17.1 per cent came to know about hospitals from their relatives and 8.7 per cent people got information from Ex–patients.

B. Factors Influencing the Selection of Hospitals

1) Out of the 10 factors influencing the selection of hospitals, Augmented facilities and Care in the hospital has the mean rank of 3.77 which is the lowest one. Lowest mean rank means it had the highest preference. So Augmented facilities and care in the hospital was the most

dominant factor that influenced the preference of the patient to make a choice. Doctors Qualification is the second dominant factor. Advice of Ex- Patients, family members, friends and relatives who have taken treatment earlier had least preference as it hadthe highest mean score.

2) As per the mean rank matrix of Mann Whitney U test, Augmented facilities and Care available in the hospital among all hospitals, the lowest mean rank went to private sector hospitals, which shows that when compared to government hospitals, private sector hospitals had better augmented facilities and care available in the hospital.

3) According to the mean rank matrix of the Kruskal Walli's test, the Augmented facilities among all hospitals the lowest mean rank went to private Super-Speciality hospitals, which shows, when compared to other hospitals private Super Speciality hospitals provides better Augmented facilities than others.

C. *Factors Influencing the Satisfaction of Patients*

1) The factors affecting the satisfaction of patients of public and private sector hospitals were explained by applying the multiple discriminant analysis. From the statistics of discriminant analysis, the Wilks Lambda characterised by the chi-square was found significant (Wilks Lambda .109 with Chi–square 1202.345, $P<0.05$). So the model was found valid for interpretation. The output also gave a centroid matrix, where

the negative co-efficient belonged to Government sector hospitals and the positive co-efficient to private sector hospitals. From the standardised canonical discriminant function it was seen that the highest negative co-efficient was -2.429, the follow up process and the second highest negative co-efficient was -1.866for Intensive Care Unit facility. But the highest positive co-efficient was 1.890, for knowledge of the staff and second highest positive co-efficient was 0.697 for Cleanliness and hygiene. Therefore, it could be concluded that in Government sector hospitals, follow up process and Intensive care unit facility, and in private sector hospitals, knowledge of the staff and Cleanliness and hygiene were the critical factors, these factors created more satisfaction among patients in these two hospital sectors

2) The Variation of all the loyalty factors among different type of hospitals were tested by using MANOVA.Based on the highest mean score, it was observed that private multi-speciality hospitals has higher Cognitive, Affective and Behavioural loyalty than that of others, whereas Private medical college has a higher Intention Loyalty.From the output it was found that all the four test statistics, (Pillai's Trace, Wilks' Lambda Hotelling's Trace, Roy's Largest Root) used for Multivariate analysis provide significant F values at 5 per cent level ($p<0.05$). It can thus be concluded that there exists significant difference in the mean scores obtained for the set of variables determining patient loyalty

among the different types of hospitals under study.

3) Regarding the Patient Trust variable, it has more influence among the Semi Urban population (Mean Score 49.274). The mean score variation is found significant at 5 per cent level($P<0.05$) for all categories of residence area.

4) The core variables affecting patients' satisfaction and their impact were identified by applying stepwise Multiple Linear Regression. The influence of independent variables, related to overall satisfaction of patients is examined withthe help of Stepwise Multiple Regression model. The Model summary table shows that the value of R^2 is 0.961, which means that 96 per cent of the influence on overall satisfaction was due to the factors such as Empathy, Responsiveness, Communication, Reliability, Access and Tangibility. The value of F statistics in ANOVA was **2202.487** which is found significant at 5 per cent level, indicating that the Regression model is fitted reasonably. Further, the Co-efficient matrix of regression indicates that Empathy, Responsiveness, Communication, Reliability, Access and Tangibility influenced the overall satisfaction of the patients,as the beta coefficient of these factors were found significant (t values with $P<.05$) in all these cases. So it could be concluded that Empathy, Responsiveness, Communication, Reliability, Access and Tangibility created more satisfaction among patients.

5) Factors such as Personality, Managerial skill, Sustainable services, Operation (surgery) Facility, Infrastructure and Information technology were considered as modern Service Quality factors.The Model Summary table shows that the value of R^2 is .899, which means that 89.9 per cent of the overall satisfaction was due to the factors such as Infrastructure facility, Personality factor, Sustainable factor, Information Technology and Managerial skill. The value of F statistics in ANOVA is 969.905 which was found significant at 5 per cent level, indicates that the Regression model is fitted reasonably. Further, the co-efficient matrix of regression indicated that Infrastructure facility, Personality factor, Sustainable factor, Information Technology and Managerial skill influence the overall satisfaction of the patients, as the Beta coefficients of these factors are found significant (t values with $P<.05$) in all these cases.

D. Factors Causing Dissatisfaction among Patients

1) Various problems faced by patients of public and private sector hospitals were explained by applying Multiple Discriminant Analysis. From the statistics of Discriminant analysis, the Wilks Lambda characterised by the chi-square was found significant (Wilks Lambda .036 with Chi–square 1797.272, $P<0.05$). So the model was found valid for interpretation. The output also gave a centroid matrix, where the negative co-efficient belonged to Government sector hospitals and the positive co-efficient to private sector hospitals. From the standardised

Canonical Discriminant function, it was seen that the highest negative co-efficient was-**11.634,** forImproper diagnosing of disease and the second highest negative co-efficient was **-4.304,** for poor quality of treatment. But the highest positive co-efficient was **9.696** for Lack of expert (specialist) doctors and second highest positive co-efficient was **9.344** for Lack of diagnostic amenities and equipment. Therefore, it could be concluded that in Government sector hospitals,Improper diagnosing of disease and poor quality of treatment and in private sector, Lack of expert (specialist) doctors and Lack of diagnostic amenities and equipments were the critical factors, these factors created more dissatisfaction among patients in these two hospital sectors.

5.3 Testing of Hypotheses

1. There is no significant difference in the factors affecting the selection of hospitals by the patients of hospitals in Kerala

This hypothesis was tested with the Friedman Chi-square test which provided a value of 1619.757 which was statistically significant at 5 per cent level of significance ($p=0.000<0.05$). Therefore, the null hypotheses is rejected with the conclusion that there is significant difference in the factors affecting the selectionby the patients of Government and Private hospitals.

2. There is no significant difference in the augmented facilities and care available for the patients of different hospitals

The KruskalWalli's test was applied to validate this hypothesis and the output showed that the value of Chi-square was significant at 5 per cent level (value of Chi-square = 46.212 with P= .000<.05). So, the null hypotheses is rejected with the conclusion that there is difference in the augmented facilities and care available for the patients of different hospitals.

3. There is no significant difference in the factors responsible for the satisfaction of patients of Private and Government Hospitals

This hypotheses was validated by applying theMultiple Discriminant analysis and the Wilk's Lambda characterised by Chi–square was found significant at 5 per cent level of significance (P=.000<.05). Therefore, this null hypothesis was rejected with the conclusion that there is significant difference in the factors responsible for the satisfaction of patients of Private and Government Hospitals.

4. There is no significant variation in the mean scores obtained for the set of variablesdescribing the loyaltyacrossvarioustypes of hospitals.

This hypothesis was tested with MANOVA and from the output it was clear that all the four test statistics (Pillai's Trace, Wilks' Lambda,Hotelling's Trace, Roy's Largest Root) used for multivariate analysis provide significant F values at 5 per cent level (p<0.05). Hence the null hypothesis is rejected. It can thus be concluded that there exists significant difference in the mean scores obtained for the set of variables determining patient loyalty among the different types of hospitals under study.

5. There is no significant dependence between overall satisfaction of patients and the core service factors such as Empathy, Responsiveness Communication, Reliability, Access and Tangibility

The influence of independent variables relating to the overall satisfaction of patients was examined with the help of Stepwise Multiple Regression model. The co-efficient matrix of regression indicated that Empathy, Responsiveness, Communication, Reliability, Access and Tangibility influenced the overall satisfaction of the patients, asthe Beta coefficient of these factors was found significant (t values with P<.05) in all these cases, thereby rejecting the null hypotheses.

6. There is no significant difference in the factor responsible for the dissatisfaction of patients of Private and Government Hospitals

This hypothesis was validated by applying Multiple Discriminant analysis and Wilks Lambda characterised by the Chi-square. It was found significant (Wilks Lambda .036 with Chi-square 1797.272, P=.000<0.05). Hence the null hypothesis was rejected by concluding that there was significant difference in the factor responsible for the dissatisfaction ofpatients of Private and Government Hospitals.

5.4 Conclusion

In the Research work, attempt has been made to analyse the level of Service Quality among patients of Government and Private Sector hospitals.

1) Among the selected patients, themajority were female and they had educational qualification upto SSLC and the majority of the patients are youngsters in the age group of 20-30.
2) The majority of the patients were from urban area and majority among them have income between Rs. 2,00,001-5,00,000.
3) A large number of patients preferred hospitals in the urban areas and the majority of them came to hospital for surgical needs and majority of the selected patients visited hospitals twice in a month.
4) The augmented facilities and care available in the hospitals were considered as the most dominant factor that influenced patients in the selection of hospitals. Among government and private hospitals, private super speciality hospitals provided better augmented care and facilities.
5) In Government hospitals, follow up process and Intensive Care Unit (ICU) facility were the critical factors that caused satisfaction, whereas it was knowledge of the staff and cleanliness and hygiene in the case of private sector hospitals.
6) Patients of Private Multi-Speciality hospital had higher cognitive, affective and behavioural

loyalty whereas patients of private medical colleges had higher intention loyalty.

7) Patients Trust variable was foundto havemore influence among semi urban Population. It means that patients in semi urban area were more conscious about the trust-worthiness of the hospitals. Rural patients were not much concerned about the trust factors of the hospitals.

8) It is found that among core service variables, Empathy, Responsiveness Communication, Reliability, Access and Tangibility created more satisfaction among patients.

9) Among the facilities available (Modern Service Qualityvariables) in the hospitals Personality, Managerial skill Sustainable Services, Operation (surgery) facility offered more satisfaction to the patients.

10) In the Government sector, improper diagnosis and poor quality of treatment caused dissatisfaction among patients whereas in the case of private hospitals lack of specialist doctors and diagnostic amenities and equipment were the factors causing dissatisfaction

11) From the study it is found that there is significant difference in the factors affecting the selection of hospitals, and that it was the provision for augmented facilities, in both sectors of hospitals,

12) Loyalty factors and Dissatisfying factorswere also significantly different in both the sectors of hospitals.

5.5 Recommendations

1) Facilities in the hospitals are considered as attracting forces and it is considered as a factor that influences the satisfaction level. Hospitals in rural areas should improve their facilities so as to attract the patients. Surgical facilities such as operation theatre and post-operative care should be improved. Patients who are in need of surgery are approaching hospitals in urban area because of improved facilities and better post-operative care. Hospitals in the rural areas should take measures to improve their surgery related facilities.

2) Augmented means enhanced version of any service. Government hospitals should give better augmented facilities and care to their patients. Facilities in most government hospitals are not upto the level. They are only giving basic facilities. But patients are expecting an enhanced level of service. Government hospitals should give better augmented facilities and care to their patients so as to attract and maintain the satisfaction level of their patients.

3) Satisfaction of the patients mainly depends on the nursing care they get from the hospitals. When we are sick, we expect personalised care and support. Hospitals in both sectors should take measures to improve Nursing care, for this hospitals should employ more nursing staff and they should be treated well.

4) Doctors' competence and expertise is a prerequisite for maintaining satisfaction of patients. Doctors in both sectors should maintain

their competence. Private hospitals should employ more competent and qualified doctors. Doctors in Government/Public sector should show more sincerity and commitment towards their patients.

5) After consulting the doctors, patients prefer to get their medicines from the hospital itself. In our hospitals a majority of the medicines prescribed by the doctors are not available in the pharmacy and we have to buy it from other medical shops. This will create a dissatisfaction among patients.Pharmacy Facility in both sectors of hospitals should be improved.

6) Loyalty is considered as an indicator of Service Quality. Loyalty towards government hospitals is very low, as compared to private sector hospitals. People don't feel loyalty towards Government hospitals as their services are not upto the level. Government hospitals should improve their loyalty level by improving their infrastructure facilities, nursing care, doctors' competence, etc.

7) Patients trust toward hospitals shows the trustworthiness of the hospitals. Hospitals should givea feel to their patients that they are honest and that patients can believe them. Hospitals should take measures to improve patients' trust.

8) Government hospitals should improve their diagnosis process and also the quality of treatment. The diagnosis process in the case of Government hospitals is very pathetic; patients

of Government hospitals has to depend private laboratories for proper diagnosis.

9) By implementing some marketing strategies and by some gimmicks, private hospitals are maintaining their patients, but the patients are not much satisfied with the available doctors; they are expecting more specialised doctors. Also, hospitalsshould improve the diagnostic amenities.

10) The health sector of Kerala is dominated by private sector hospitals. Eventhough government is pumping huge amount in the health sector, people are not much benefited from the public health care sector. The Government should take measures to improve the public health care system.

5.6 Scope for Further Study

1) A study on the Promotional Strategies of private hospitals in Kerala.

2) Service Quality and Customer Satisfaction of Ayurveda Hospitals in Kerala.

Bibliography

Aaker, D. A. & Jacobson, R. (1994), "The financial information content of perceived service quality", Journal of Marketing Research, *e31*, May, pp. 191-201.

Aaron, A. Abuosi & Roger A. Atinga, (2013), "Service Quality in healthcare Institutions: Establishing the gaps for policy action", International Journal of Health Care Quality Assurance, *26* (5), pp. 481 – 492.

Ahenkan, A. & Aduo-Adjei, K. (2017), Predictors of Patient Satisfaction with Quality of Healthcare in University Hospitals in Ghana, Hospital Practices and Research, *2* (1): pp 9-14.

Ahmed, Rizwan & Sameera, Hina, (2011),Assessing the Service Quality of selected hospitals in Karachi, based on SERVQUAL model. Pakistan Business Review, July 2011, pp. 266-314.

Ahmed, S. Tarique, K.M. & Arif, I. (2017), "Service quality, patient satisfaction and loyalty in the Bangladesh healthcare sector", International Journal of health care quality assurance, *30*(5): pp 477-488.

Ahuja, Markanday; Mahlawat, Seema & Masood, Rana Zehra, (2011), "Study on Service Quality Management with SERVQUAL Model: An Empirical Study of Government/NGOs hospitals in Haryana", Indian Journal of Communication and Management Studies,*11* (2), (March 2011) pp. 310-318.

Aiello A., Garman A. & Morris B.S. (2003),"Patient satisfaction with nursing care: A multilevel analysis", Journal of Quality Management in Health Care, *12* (3): pp 187- 191.

Aiswarya S, (2015), Impact of Service Quality on Customer Satisfaction In the Health Care Sector (With Reference to Hospitals in Bangalore), Published Ph.D Thesis SRM University,

Ajam, M., Sadeghifar, J., Anjomshoa, M., Mahmoudi, S., Honarvar, H. &Mousavi, S.M. (2014), "Assessing quality of healthcare service by the SERVQUAL model: A case study of a field hospital", Journal of Military Medicine, *15* (4): pp 273–279.

Ajarmah, B.S. & Hashem, T.N. (2015),"Patient Satisfaction evaluation on Hospitals; Comparison Study between accredited and non accredited hospitals in Jordan", European Scientific Journal, *11* (32): pp 298-314.

Akbar, F.H. & Jaya, M.T. (2017),"Relationship between Service Quality on Public Health Center and Patient Satisfaction", Global Journal of Health Science, *9* (7): pp 96-102.

Ali, S.S. & Ahmed, F. (2010),"Measuring Indian Patients' Satisfaction: a case of Private Hospitals", Portuguese Journal of Management Studies, *15* (3) pp 303-329.

Ali, S.S. Kaur, R. Pande, M.J.C. & Ahmad, F. (2014),"Service quality gap approach: A case of Indian customer's satisfaction of private banks", International Journal of Business Excellence, *7* (4): pp. 429–453.

Alijanzadeh, M. Moosaniaye Zare, S. A. Rajaee, R. Mohammad Ali M.F.S. Asefzadeh, S. Alijanzadeh, M. &Gholami, S. (2016), Comparison Quality of Health Services between Public and Private Providers: The Iranian People's Perspective, Electron Physician, *8* (9).

Aliman, N.K. & Mohamad, W.N. (2016), Linking Service Quality, Patients' Satisfaction and Behavioral Intentions: An investigation on Private Healthcare in Malaysia, Procedia - Social and Behavioral Sciences, *224* (2016): pp 141–148.

Allena Tasneem, Sundas Shaukat, & Fatima Amin, *(2010),* "Patient Satisfaction; A Comparative Study atTeaching versus DHQ Level Hospital in Lahore, Pakistan". Journal of Pharmaceutical Sciences and *Research, 2 (11),2010, PP 767-774, ISSN.09 75-1459.*

Amira Elleuch (2005), "Patient Satisfaction in Japan", International Journal of Health Care Quality Assurance, 21 (7), 2005.

Amitabh Dey (2015), Assessing the Quality of Service and Delivery Standards: A Study of Selected Upscale Restaurants in Kolkata, Published Ph.D Thesis, School of Tourism & Hospitality Services Management (SOTHSM) Indira Gandhi National Open University, New Delhi.

Anjali Patwardhan (2009), "A Retrospective on Access to health care", International Journal of Health Care Quality Assurance, 20 (6), 2007 pp. 494-505 Emerald Group Publishing Limited.

Ansuman Samal (2018), Comparative Study on Service Quality in Public, Published Ph.D thesis, Siksha O Anusandhan (Deemed to be University), Bhubaneswar, Odisha

Arasanamand, Prachayaporn, Yousapronpaiboon, &Khanchitpol, (2014),"The relationship between Service Quality and Customer Satisfaction of pharmacy departments in Public hospitals". Journal of Basic and Applied Science Research, *4* (1), pp. 144-151.

Archana Patel, Vijay Thawani&KundaGharpure, (2003).World Health Organisation, (Health Action International) In Medicine Pricing Affordability and Availability in Maharashtra.

Ari Mawachofi & Stephen L. Walston (2011), "Factors affecting Nurses' Perceptions of patient safety", International Journal of Health Care Quality Assurance, *24* (4), pp. 274-283.

Ashok Sahni & Prof. Hony, (1992), Management of Outpatient Services, Hospital and Health Administration, Second edition, Yem Yes Printers, Bangalore, 1992, p 18.

Ashok Vikhe-Patil, K.V. Somasundaram, & R. C. Goyal (2002)."Current Health scenario in rural India", Australian Journal of Rural Health Vol.10, page 129–135.

B. Hannah (2012), A Study on Service Quality of Government Hospital And Mission Hospital In Tiruchirapalli, Tamilnadu, Published Thesis, Bharathidasan University.

Bahadori, Mohammadkarim; Raadabadi Mehdi; Jamebozorgi, Majidheidari; Salesi Mahmood &

Ravangard, Ramin (2014), Nephro Urology Monthly, Nephrourolmon. *6* (5).

Berry L. L., Parasuraman A, &Zeithaml VA, (1988). The service quality puzzle, Business Horizons, p-36–44.

Bhore Committee, (1946), "The Health Survey and development"

Bolton R.N., & James H.D. (1991), "A longitudinal analysis of the impact of service changes on customer attitudes", Journal of Marketing , 55: pp. 1–9.

Bopp KD. (1990) "How patients evaluate the quality of ambulatory medical encounters". Journal Healthcare Marketing; 10: pp. 6–15.

Boshoff, C. & Gray, B., (2001) "The relationship between Service Quality, Customer Satisfaction and Buying Intentions in the Private Hospital Industry", South African Journal of Business Management,pp 35

Bowers, M.R., Swan, J.E., & Koehler, W., (1994) "What Attributes Determine Quality and Satisfaction with Health Care Delivery?", Health Care Management Review, *19* (4).

Brahmbhatt, Mamta, Baser, Narayan, & Joshi, Nisarg, (2011), "Adapting SERVQUAL scale to Hospital services: An Empirical investigation of patients' perceptions of service quality". ZENITH International Journal of Multidisciplinary Research, *1* (8), pp. 27-42.

Brown, S.W. & Swartz, T.W., (1989) "A Gap Analysis of Professional Service Quality", Journal of Marketing, *53* (4).

Byju K.P.M (2014), Service Quality in Healthcare: A comparative study of Private and Public sector healthcare services, Published Ph.D Thesis, Pondicherry University

C. Jothi Baskara Mohan, (2009). A Study of Human Resource Development Practices and Patient Care Quality in Health Care Services with Special Reference to Government Hospitals in Tamilnadu, Published Thesis, Madurai Kamraj University

Capra, S., Wright, O., Sardie, M., Bauer, J. & Askew, D. (2005), "The Acute Foodservice Patient Satisfaction Interview Schedule: the development of a valid and reliable tool to measure patient satisfaction with acute care hospital foodservices", Foodservice Research International, *16*, pp. 1-14.

Choi, K.S., Lee, H., Kein, C. & Lee, S., (2005), "The Service Quality Dimensions and Patient Satisfaction Relationship in South Korea: Comparison Across Gender, Age and Type of Service", The Journal of Service Marketing, *19*(3), 2005.

Coddington, D., Fischer, E., Moore, K., & Clarke, R.(2007), "Beyond Managed Care–How Consumers and Technology are Changing the future of Health Care", Jossey-Bass, San Francisco, CA,2007.

Conel C., & Fletcther E.A.A, (1985), "An analysis of service quality at a student health centre", International Journal of Healthcare Quality Assurance 1985; 14: pp. 260–267.

David Camilleri & Mark O Callaghan, (2003), "Comparing Public and Private Hospital Care Service Quality", International Journal of Health Care Quality, *11*(4), 2003.

David P. Paul & Earl D (1995)."An analysis of thehospital Marketing Relationship in the healthcare industry",

The Journal of Healthcare Marketing 10(1), pp 35-49.

Devabakan, N., & Akgarayli, M.(2012), "The Usage of SERVQUAL scores for the Measurement of Quality of Perceived Service in Health Facilities and Implementation of Private Altimordu Hospital", Journal of Institute of Social Sciences, 5 (1), 2012.

Dogra, Ajay Kumar (2019), Customer Orientation and Service Quality Practices in hospital industry, a study of Public and Private hospitals in North India, Published Thesis, Panjab University, Chandigarh.

Donabedian, A (1980), Explorations in Quality Assessment and Monitoring. Ann Arbor. MI: Health Administration Press.

Dr. Chandrakumar Sedamkar, (2011), Studyof Health Management Among the Aged.Southern Economist, 49th year of publication, 49 (21), March 1, 2011, pp.38 -42.

Dr. Shridhar Vaman Sherigar (June-2005). "An Analytical study of the Quality of Patient services in some selected Hospitals in Mumbai."

Dube and Laurette (2003) What's missing from Patient – Centered Care?, Marketing health services, Spring 2003, 23(1), p. 30.

Dursun, Y. & Cerci, M. (2012), "Perceived Service Quality: A Study on Patient Satisfaction and Behavioural Factors", Journal of Community Health, 24(1), 2012.

Eugine Franco, C. (2008), Marketing of Professional Services with particular reference to hospitals in Kanyakumari district, Published Ph.D Thesis, Manonmaniam Sundaranar University

Francesca, Garrard & Harini Narayan, (2013) "Assessing Obstetric patient experience: a SERVQUAL Interview Schedule", International Journal of Health Care Quality Assurance, *26* (7), pp.582 – 592.

G.J. Fagare (1991). Thesis titled "Impact and Assessment of National Health Policy with special reference to Chandgadtaluka."

Gaba, D., Howard S. & Small, S. (1995) Situation awareness in anesthesiology. Human Factors, pp. 20-31.

Glady Eswara Raj S. (2019) Patients perception towards the services provided by the hospitals of Tirunelveli District. Published Ph.D. Thesis Manomanian Sundaranar University

Gooding, S.K.S., (1995), "Quality, Sacrifice and Value in Hospital Choice", Journal of Health Care Marketing, 15 (4), 1995.

Grandzol, J.R., & Gershown, M., (2010), "Which TQM Practices Really Matter: An Empirical Investigation", Quality Measurement Journal, *4*(1),

Gronroos. C., (1990) A service quality model and its marketing implications. Eur J Marketing 1990; 18:pp. 36–44.

Hausman (2004), "Professional Service Relationship: A Multi Context Study of Factors Impacting Satisfaction, Repatronization and Recommendation", The Journal of Service Marketing, 17(2&3), 2004.

Hofmann, M. & Von Rosenstiel, L. (Eds), (1988), Motivations Management in Functional Management, Springer, Berlin, pp 14-19.

Honkan, G.G (2012) Southern Economist, Golden Jubilee year of publication,50 (9), Feb 1, 2012, pp. 31-36.

Hussein, M. Al Borie, Amal M. & Sheikh Damanhouri, (2013) "Patients' Satisfaction of Service Quality in Saudi hospitals: a SERVQUAL analysis", International Journal of Health Care Quality Assurance, 26 (1), pp.20 – 30.

Hwang, L., Eves, A. & Desombre, T., (2009) "Gap Analysis of Patient Meal Service Perceptions", International Journal of Health Care Quality Assurance, 16 (9), 2003.

I. Irulappan (2014) Service Quality in Health Care Centres: A Comparative Study between Government and Private Sector Hospitals in Dindigul, Published Thesis, Madurai Kamaraj University.

Jeen Su Lim & Ron Zallocco (1997) "Consumer Attitude toward Health Care Marketing Practices: Acomparison of hospitals vs physicians"- The Jounal of Healthcare Marketing 12 (1), pp. 91-108.

Johan Hellings, Ward Schrooten & Niek Klazinga (2007), "Challenging patient safety culture: survey results", International Journal of Health Care Quality Assurance *20*(7), 2007 pp. 620-632.

Jr. J. J. Cronin & S A. Taylor (1992). "Measuring Service Quality: A Re-examination and Extension". Journal of Marketing, *56* (3),pp. 55-68.

K. Nithyanandam (2015) 'Service Quality of Life Insurance Corporation of India', Published Ph.D Thesis, University of Madras.

Kirubaharan, M. (2012), A Study on the Quality of Healthcare Service and Patients' Satisfaction towards Apollo hospitals in Tamilnadu, Published Thesis, Bharathiar University, Coimbatore

Kovai V., Rao, Holden B, Sannapaneni K, Bhattacharya SK, & Khanna R (2010) "Comparison of PatientSatisfaction with services of vision Centers in rural areas of Andhra Pradesh, India", Indian Journal of Ophthalmology, 2010 Sep–Oct; 58(5); pp. 407-413.

Kui-Son Choi, Hanjoon Lee, Chankon Kim and Suhbee Lee, (2002) "The Service Quality Dimensions and Patient Satisfaction Relationship in South Korea: Comparisons Across Agenda, Age and Types of Services", Journal of Services Marketing, *19* (3), 2002.

Kumar Chunduri (2011), The Service Quality Gap Analysis – A Study On Selected Hospitals in Hyderabad AcharyaNagarjuna University, Andhra Pradesh.

Kumar, Arun; Manjunath, Chethan, (2012), "Service quality at Hospital- a study of Apollo Hospital in Mysore" IOSR Journal of Business and Management, *4*(I), (Sept-Oct 2012), pp. 01-07.

K. Vaidyanathan, "ESI Scheme a Waste, Fear Junior Executives", The Indian Express, *128*, p.8, October 13, 2009.

Lam, S.S.K, (1997) "SERVQUAL: A Tool for Measuring Patients Opinions of Hospital Service Quality in Hong Kong", Total Quality Management, *8*(4), 1997.

Lamber, D.M., Marmorstein, H. & Sharma, A. (1990), "The Accuracy of Salespersons Perceptions of Their Customers: Conceptual Examination and an Empirical Study". Journal of Personal Selling & Sales Management, 10 (8), pp 1-9

Lim, P.C. & Tang, N.K.H., (2003), "A Study of Patient's Expectations and Satisfaction in Singapore

Hospitals", International Journal of Health Care Quality Assurance, *13* (7), pp.290-299.

Manoj Kumar (2016) Service Quality Gaps in Retail Outlets in Haryana, Published Thesis Guru Jambheshwar University of Science & Technology

Maria Helena Vinagre & Jose Neves (2002), "The Influence of Service Quality and Patients' Emotion on Satisfaction", International Journal of Health Care Quality Assurances, *21* (1), pp.87-103.

Marino & Phyllis, B(2003)., 'We Are the Voice of the Customer', Marketing Health services, summer2003, 23(2), p 52.

Melvin F. Hall (1995) "Patient satisfaction of aequiscence" The Jounal of Healthcare Marketing,*15*.

Monisha (2018) Customers' Perception of Quality Delivery of E-Services in Banks, Published Thesis, MaharshiDayanand University, Rohtak

Mr. Jaswal Ashish Rajendra (2017). A study on consumer's perception towards Service Quality in private hospitals. Published Ph.D. thesis, SavitribaiPhule University, Pune

Ms. Anjali A Deshpande (2011) Yeshwant Rao Chavan Maharashtra Open University, Nashik, "Telemedicine-A Ray of Hope for Millionsof Indians" Southern Economist, 50 (6), July 15, 2011, pp.No.35 -38.

Narver. J. & Slater, S. (1990). "The Effect of a Market Orientation on BusinessProfitability", *Journal of Marketing, 54*(4), pp 20-35.

Nidhi Malik (2019) Service Quality in Technical Education System: A Study of Polytechnics In Haryana,

Published Thesis, Maharshi Dayanand University, Rohtak

Nishikant Waikar (2010), A Study of Service Quality Assessment in Hospitals, Published Ph.D Thesis, Institute of Management Studies, Devi Ahilya Vishwavidhyalaya, Indore.

Nishikant Waikar (2010), A study of Service Quality assessment in hospitals Published Ph.D Thesis, Institute of Management studies, Devi Ahilya Vishwavidhyalaya, Indore

Norazah MohdSuki; Jennifer Chiam Chwee Lian & Norbayah Mohd Suki, (2011) "Do Patients' Perceptions exceed their expectations in Private Healthcare settings?" International Journal of Health Care Quality Assurance, *24*(1), pp.42 – 56.

P.S. Kabaly (2011) Medical Tourists' Perception Of Service Quality In Indian Hospitals: A Study With Specific Reference to Sultanate of Oman, Published Ph.D Thesis, Alagappa University.

Parasuraman, A., Zeithaml V.A., & Berry L.L., (1993). "A multiple items scale for measuring consumer perceptions of service quality". Journal of Retailing; *66*, pp-12–40.

Parasuraman, A., Valarie A. Zeithaml, & Leonard L. Berry (1988), "SERVQUAL: A Multiple-item Scale for Measuring Consumer Perceptions of Service Quality," Journal of Retailing, 64/1 (Spring), pp 12-40.

Parasuraman, V. Zeithaml & L. Berry, (1985) "A Conceptual Model of Service Quality and Its Implications for Future Research", Journal of Marketing, *49* (Fall), 1985.

Pragati Chadda (2017), Service Quality and Patient Satisfaction with Reference to Multi Specialty Hospitals. Published thesis Kurukshetra University, Kurukshetra

R. David Rajesh (2017) A Study on Linkage between Service Quality, Service Fairness and Service Loyalty in Hospitals in Madurai, Published Thesis, Periyar University

Raja Irfan Sabir; Nabila, Noor; Wasim, Ahmad; Farhan, Qaisar; Hussnain, Kamil&Naima, Khurshid; (2014), "Impact of Service Quality on Patient's Satisfaction using SERVQUAL': A comparison of Combined Military, Private and Government Hospitals of Pakistan", Journal of Basic and Applied Scientific Research, *4* (1), pp. 144-151.

RamaiahItumalla (2014) Evaluation of Service Quality Management in Indian Hospitals: A Study of Select Hospitals Published Thesis, University of Hyderabad.

Raman Sharma, Meenakshi Sharma, & R.K. Sharma. (2011) "The Patient Satisfaction Study in a MultiSpecialty Tertiary Level Hospital, PGIMER, Chandigarh, India". Leadership in Health Services. 24 (1), 2011 pp 64-73.

Rethina Sivakumar, G (2012) A Study on Mediating Effects on Service Loyalty On Healthcare Services in Tamilnadu India, Published Thesis Bharathidasan Institute of Management

Rina C. Dave, (2013) Service Quality and Customer Satisfaction in Health Care Sector: An Empirical Study on Selected Private Hospitalsof Gujarat. Published Thesis, Sardar Patel University, Vallabh Vidyanagar

Robert F. Krampf. & Darryl W. Miller (1993), "Hospital Successes and Failures Indicate Change in Hospital Marketing", Journal of Hospital Marketing *7* (2), pp 11-19.

Rupal Kantilal Khambhati (2018) Service Quality Measurement of Public Healthcare Facility: A Comparative Study on Urban and Rural Consumers of Surat District, Published Thesis, Gujarat Technological University Ahmedabad,

S.P. Murugan (2017) A Study On Patients' Awareness, Satisfaction And Quality Measurement of Health Care Services Provided By Private Multi – Speciality Hospitals In Coimbatore District, Tamil Nadu Published Ph.D Thesis, Periyar University, Salem.

Sarhani Chakraborthy and Kein Frick (2013), "Factors Influencing Private Health Prider's Technical Quality of Care for Acute Respiratory Infection among UnderFive Children in Rural West Bengal, India", Social Science and Medicine, *55* (5), pp.1579-1587.

Seltman & Kent (2002), 'The Final Word on Patient Satisfaction' Marketing Health services, Summer2002, *23(2), p 3.*

Sindhya R (2016) Evaluation of Patients' Expected and Perceived Quality of Hospital Services Using SERVQUAL Approach in Southern Part of Tamilnadu, Published Thesis, Anna University.

Sivakumar, M (2010). A study on Evaluation of Healthcare services in corporate hospitals with special reference to Madurai, Published Ph.D Thesis, MaduraiKamraj University.

Solaiyappan, Annamalai; Jayakrishnan, Jothi; Velmani, Sethu, (2011), Quality Measurement for hospital

Services, 3rd International Conference on Information and Financial Engineering, IPERD, *12* (2011), pp. 246-250.

Somnath Chatterjee (2015). A Study of Healthcare Management System in West Bengal With Special Reference to The District of Burdwan, University of Burdwan, Burdwan

Srinivasa Rao (2011), Marketing of Hospital Services, Published Thesis, Acharya Nagarjuna University.

Sritharan, V, (2014), "Measuring Service Quality Dimensions: an Empirical Study of Private Hospitals in Jaffna District, Sri Lanka". Journal of Marketing and Consumer Research, *3*.

Subramanyam, V (1997), "Quality of care at Community Hospitals", Economic and Political Weekly, XXXII, (37), September, 1997, pp. 20-21.

Sudha. S.R (2012) "Private & Public Partnership in Healthcare services in India" Southern Economist, December 15, 2012, pp. 42-46.

Sundaravadivelu, A.B. (2013) Service Quality Strategies of Medical services - A study with reference to Private hospitals in Chennai, Published Ph.D thesis, University of Madras

Syed Sadd Andaleeb (2008), "Determinants of Customer Satisfaction with Hospitals: A Managerial Model", International Journal of Health Care Quality Assurance, *11*(6), 2008.

Taner, T. and J Antony, (2013), "Comparing Public and Private Hospital Care Service Quality in Turkey", International Journal of Health Care Quality Assurance, *19* (2), pp. 1-9.

Teamur Aghamolaei; Tasnim Eghba Eftekhaari; Shideh Rafati; Kobra Kahnouji; Shamsieh Ahangari; Mohammad Esmaeil Shahrzad; Ataollah Kahnouji & Seyedeh Hamideh Hoseini (2014) Service Quality assessment of a referral hospital in Southern Iran with SERVQUAL technique: Patients' Perspective, BMC Health Services Research, 2014, pp 14-32.

Thomas and Richard K. (2002), 'Treating patients like Customers' Marketing Health services, Summer 2002,23 (2), p 38.

Tse DK, Wilton PC. (1988) "Models of customer satisfaction formation". Journal of Marketing Research; 25: 204–212.

V. Andal (2016), Customer Service Quality – Relationship and Satisfaction (CSQ – R&S) In Health Care and Hospital Services in Chennai City, Published Thesis, Savitribai Phule University, Pune.